A BEGINNER'S GUIDE TO
American Mah Jongg

How to Play the Game and Win

Elaine Sandberg

FOREWORD BY TOM SLOPER

TUTTLE Publishing

Tokyo | Rutland, Vermont | Singapore

"Books to Span the East and West"

Tuttle Publishing was founded in 1832 in the small New England town of Rutland, Vermont [USA]. Our core values remain as strong today as they were then—to publish best-in-class books which bring people together one page at a time. In 1948, we established a publishing outpost in Japan—and Tuttle is now a leader in publishing English-language books about the arts, languages and cultures of Asia. The world has become a much smaller place today and Asia's economic and cultural influence has grown. Yet the need for meaningful dialogue and information about this diverse region has never been greater. Over the past seven decades, Tuttle has published thousands of books on subjects ranging from martial arts and paper crafts to language learning and literature—and our talented authors, illustrators, designers and photographers have won many prestigious awards. We welcome you to explore the wealth of information available on Asia at **www.tuttlepublishing.com**.

Published by Tuttle Publishing, an imprint of Periplus Editions (HK) Ltd.

www.tuttlepublishing.com

Copyright © 2007, 2010 by Elaine Sandberg

Library of Congress Cataloging-in-Publication Data

Sandberg, Elaine.
  Beginner's guide to American mah jongg : how to play the game and win / Elaine Sandberg ; foreword by Tom Sloper.
— 1st ed.
    124 p. : col. ill. ; 23 cm.
  ISBN 0-8048-3878-X (pbk. : alk. paper)
1. Mah jong. I. Title.
GV1299.M3S28 2007
795.3'4—dc22
                           2006029920
ISBN 978-0-8048-3878-8

Distributed by:

North America, Latin America & Europe
Tuttle Publishing
364 Innovation Drive
North Clarendon,
VT 05759-9436 U.S.A.
Tel: 1 (802) 773-8930;
Fax: 1 (802) 773-6993
info@tuttlepublishing.com
www.tuttlepublishing.com

Asia Pacific
Berkeley Books Pte. Ltd.
3 Kallang Sector #04-01,
Singapore 349278
Tel: (65) 6741 2178
Fax: (65) 6741 2179
Inquiries@periplus.com.sg
www.tuttlepublishing.com

First edition
27 26 25 24
25 24 23 22
Printed in China   2405CM

TUTTLE PUBLISHING® is a registered trademark of Tuttle Publishing, a division of Periplus Editions (HK) Ltd.

A Beginner's Guide to
AMERICAN MAH JONGG

＊☾ ☽＊

I wish to extend, to each and every student I have taught over the past years, the most sincere *thank you!* You are the impetus, the reason for this book. I have learned more about teaching mah jongg from you than any other source. You have given me important insights into what, when and how to teach, and into the importance of explaining clearly and simply, using a variety of teaching tools. This book is a reflection of all I have gained from you.

Mah jongg is exciting, competitive, sociable—and fun.

❧ CONTENTS ☙

Foreword *by Tom Sloper* 9

How to Use This Book 11

CHAPTER 1

What Is Mah Jongg? Introduction to the Game 13

CHAPTER 2

Unraveling the Mystery of the Tiles 21

Quiz and Answers 34

CHAPTER 3

Cracking the Code 35

Exercise: Learn the Hands on the Card 52

Quiz and Answers 53

CHAPTER 4

Construction Project: The Wall 57

Quiz and Answers 64

CHAPTER 5

What Do I Do Now? How to Select Your Hand 67

Exercise: Select Your Hand 76

CHAPTER 6

Cha, Cha, Charleston 77
Exercise: Select Your Hand, & The Charleston 87
Quiz and Answers 88

CHAPTER 7

The Play's the Thing 89
Exercise: Solitaire Mah Jongg 104
Quiz and Answers 105

CHAPTER 8

Play to Win: Strategies 107
Strategy Practice and Answers 114

Appendix A—Mah Jongg Sets: Where to Purchase a Set
    & How to Update Old Sets 117

Appendix B—How to Obtain Mah Jongg Cards 119

Glossary 121

❧ FOREWORD ❧

Of the many mah jongg variants extant today, American mah jongg is unique. The single most popular variant in North America, it's also the least well documented.

Prior to the publication of this book, you could not find anything about the American game in bookstores. Instead, what you would have found were descriptions of various modern Chinese regional variants, the classic Chinese rules (still played today only in Europe), or the rules played in Australia or the United Kingdom. Modern American rules, and, especially, strategy tips, were simply nowhere to be found on the store shelves.

As a result, many players of the American game had to learn by osmosis. They learned from other players who had learned by osmosis. The rare player who was willing to teach a novice rarely explained, or even knew, the details of the official rules. These mentors often used unofficial table rules, which were then propagated as "the way it's done."

Whatever the reason for this unhappy situation, there was clearly a need. This book fills it. Elaine Sandberg explains in clear language how to read the card and how to develop a beginning strategy. Finally, novices have a tool to help them through the learning curve so they can enjoy this uniquely American game that has fascinated and beguiled players since 1937.

Use this book to learn the basics and to develop your strategy, as an adjunct to the rulebook from the National Mah Jongg League. Do the exercises. They really work. But above all, have fun. Armed with the knowledge gained from this book, you can join a game with other players, confident that you are up to the challenge. And it is a challenge—a challenge to be embraced, for it keeps the little gray cells of our brains active, alive, and entertained.

Tom Sloper
Game Designer, Producer, Consultant
http://www.sloperama.com/mjfaq.html

✿ HOW TO USE THIS BOOK ✿

Mah jongg is an exciting game, loads of fun, and many people who play it get addicted to it. But learning the game can be challenging.

This book is key to ensuring that your learning experience is easy. It starts with the basics and introduces new information, chapter by chapter, in clear, simple to follow steps. Finally, the last and more complicated chapters help you put together everything you've learned so you can play the game and win.

- ✤ *A Beginner's Guide to American Mah Jongg* is structured so that you play as you learn. There are "Do It" icons throughout the book that lead you through the procedures, lots of illustrations and examples to clarify concepts, exercises to give you practice doing the things you need, and summaries and short quizzes to help you focus on important information in each chapter.

- ✤ You will gain greater and faster benefits from the book if you do the practice exercises and the quizzes; you will find you're able to integrate the information more easily.

- ✤ Many beginners find that reading the book a second time is very helpful. They discover concepts that were missed during the first reading, and procedures that seemed complicated at first, become simple.

- ✤ In addition, I recommend that when you begin the process of learning mah jongg, you plan to set aside a few (fun!) hours at a time for it. If you allow yourself more than a few days' break between chapters, you have a greater tendency to forget what you learned in the previous sections. You will find that learning the game is much easier if you simply plan your time regularly, on a consistent schedule. It sounds like a lot, but I must tell you that all the reports I have received from new players are the same: they were anxious to get to the next chapter because they found the game to be such fun. I hope you will too.

As well as being a "how-to" guide for the beginner, this book is useful for those who may have played the game in the past and wish to refresh their skills. Many players use it as a reference. Instructors may want to use it as a text, as I do, in addition to their other teaching tools. The book is written so that the reader can learn on his or her own to play the game, but it assumes four people will be learning and playing the game simultaneously.

In order to learn the game, you will need an American mah jongg set. Information on where to buy a set is available in Appendix A.

CHAPTER 1

What Is Mah Jongg?
Introduction to the Game

"Two-Crak, Flower, nine-Dot, Red, Take." No, it's not some coded message from outer space. It's mah jongg, the game my mom, and maybe yours, played, lo, these many years ago. I can still hear the clatter and click of the tiles, somebody calling "Mah Jongg!" and the "Ooohs" and "Aaahs" that followed, the buzz and the laughter. And I have fond memories of raiding the fridge the next day to enjoy the leftover goodies. Today, it's still the same. People are playing mah jongg, buzzing and laughing and having fun!

I am always amused to hear people pooh-poohing mah jongg with the stereotypical phrase that it's "an old lady's game." One of my students was a typical example. "My mom used to play mah jongg two or three times a week. She played for 30 years with the same friends and I could never understand why." That is, until she took her first lesson. She realized mah jongg is definitely not "an old lady's game," but what an interesting and challenging game it is.

Why do so many people love the game? The answer, primarily, is *it's fun!* It's simple and at the same time complex. It's competitive: you play against three other people. It's sociable: people play for hours, they eat, they talk, and they laugh. There are groups of players that have been together for decades. It takes thinking: figuring out the best plan for your individual hand, deciding how to keep others from winning, and using appropriate strategies. It's not called "The Game of a Thousand Intelligences" for nothing. It's relaxing: it allows people to focus on something completely unrelated to everyday concerns. And it's thrilling: there's nothing more exciting than when, with your heart racing, your adrenaline pumping and your palms sweating, you call "Mah Jongg!"

And on top of that, it's non-fattening and it's legal!

Families, friends, kids, clubs, parties, church groups, associations, on cruise ships, in tournaments, at vacation spas—folks play mah jongg like crazy, in almost every country you can think of, from China, Japan, and the Philippines, to Australia, Germany, Russia, and South Africa. Even though many countries have their own versions, including America, suffice it to say, the appeal of the game is undeniable and universal.

The popularity of mah jongg during the 1930s, '40s, and '50s was legendary. People from all walks of life and all parts of the country played it. With the demographic shift from city life to suburban life, the introduction of bridge, and the return to the work force by women, the popularity of mah jongg gradually faded. But today, the game of American mah jongg is making a huge comeback. Once you learn the fundamentals of the game and begin to play, you will understand why so many people love it.

So let me introduce you to mah jongg. Mah jongg originally came from China, and uses small rectangular tiles stamped with symbols and characters. The object of the game is to be the first to assemble combinations of these tiles into specific patterns that make up a hand. You assemble these combinations by picking and discarding tiles. That's the game.

But, of course, actually playing the game is not that simple. Players of American mah jongg need a card of hands. You can see what a card looks like on page 36. Without one, you can't learn or play the game, because in order to win, a player's hand must match a hand selected from the card. For learning purposes, we'll be using a card published by the National Mah Jongg League

(NMJL). The NMJL is the organization that standardized the procedures and rules of the American game and this book is based upon those procedures and rules. Everyone who plays American mah jongg follows them.

Besides the NMJL, there are other mah jongg groups that publish their own cards, such as the American Mah-Jongg Association (AMJA). Once you understand the basic elements of a card and you learn to read it, you will be able to play with a card published by any other mah jongg association; they all use the same system. For further information about the NMJL or AMJA see Appendix B.

Unfortunately, you cannot learn to play mah jongg in an hour or two. It takes awhile. There are many new ideas and concepts, a lot of things you need to remember, particularly when you first begin, and a host of do's and don'ts. But as you learn the game and begin to play, things that may have seemed difficult soon become easy. That's part of the fun of mah jongg.

> *Tip:* If you are familiar with the card game gin rummy, you have a head start in understanding mah jongg. There are differences, of course, but it's the same general idea. Instead of cards, in mah jongg you mix and pick tiles, arrange your tiles in combinations for a hand, and take turns to pick and discard tiles to make a hand. Mah jongg requires four players, while gin requires two. Gin, like Chinese mah jongg, allows the player to make up runs and combinations for a hand, but that's not the case in American mah jongg.

Because learning to play the game requires a little time and a little patience, this guide is written in an easy, conversational style. It has lots of pictures, examples, hints, tips, summaries of important information, and relevant do's and don'ts, all designed to make your learning experience easy and fun. Absorb one or two parts of the game at a time, and take as much time as you need. For beginners, reading the book a second time may clear up many ideas that, at the first reading, were challenging. You may want to read through the entire book to get a feel for the game, then go back to the beginning and start the process of learning it.

❧ History ☙

Before we begin to focus on the details of the game, let's briefly look at the origins of American mah jongg.

Mah jongg originated in China and is still played there, not only as a high-stakes gambling game, but also as a traditional family activity in many homes. There are several different interpretations of the term *mah jongg.* Loosely translated, the name means "clattering sparrows," which refers to the sound of the tiles when they are mixed or shuffled. Mah jongg is a synthesis of many different Chinese games, some using cards and some using tiles, played over the centuries. Despite stories that mah jongg is an ancient game played in Confucius' time, the game gradually evolved into the essence of Chinese mah jongg around the 1880s to 1890s.

Originally, official government edicts permitted only the Chinese elite to play, because of the fear that if the peasants played the game, they might develop their mental capacities. But with the democratization of China, in the early 1900s under the regime of China's first elected President, Sun-Yat-Sen, mah jongg's popularity quickly spread to the general Chinese population. It became "the people's game." Mah jongg was outlawed during the Mao regime because it was so closely associated with gambling. But with Mao's demise, mah jongg experienced a resurgence of popularity, and it remains one of the most popular games in China today.

Around the turn of the century in Shanghai, two British brothers named White introduced mah jongg to their English clubs and the game rapidly became popular among Westerners there. From Shanghai, it came to the United States via an American, Joseph Babcock. He had been employed in China in the oil industry and when he returned to the U.S. in early 1920, he brought the game with him. He coined the name "mah jongg" and wrote a how-to booklet, called "Rules for Mah-Jongg." It was published in San Francisco with the first printing dated September, 1920. The ninth printing appeared in

The Game of Mah-Jongg

Fig. 1 Bamboo (Tiao)

DESCRIPTION OF THE PIECES: The game is played with a set of 136 pieces, similar to dominoes, of bamboo and ivory engraved in color. There are 34 distinct, different kinds of pieces and four of each kind make up the set.

Fig. 2. Dots (Tung)

The thirty-four different kinds of pieces are made up as follows: First, there are the three suits, designated by Chinese, "Bamboo," "Dots," and "Characters," and called by Chinese, respectively, "tiao," "tung," and "wan" (see figures 1, 2 and 3). Each of these three suits runs from one to nine. Thus, the various pieces are referred to as "one tiao," "four tung," "seven wan," etc. In the three suits there are twenty-seven different kinds of pieces, four alike of each kind, making a total of 108.

In addition there are the four winds, known as the East, South, West, and North winds (see figure 4) and also the special honor pieces called

Fig. 3. Characters (Wan)

1

Babcock's Rules for

Mah-Jongg

麻雀

The Red Book of Rules

June of 1923, which gives you an idea of how quickly the popularity of the game spread. Babcock applied for a patent in 1923, sold it to Parker Brothers in 1925 and the rest, as we say, is history.

It took off like wildfire and became very popular across the country. Mah jongg, as described in Babcock's booklet, is a somewhat simplified version of the game as it was played by the Chinese. But as the game increased in popularity in America, people created their own versions, with different rules popping up helter-skelter. In 1937 the National Mah Jongg League was created to standardize the rules. Over the years, there have been a few rule changes by the

NMJL, but it is essentially the same game played in 1937 that is played today. The NMJL publishes a mah jongg card, "Standard Hands and Rules," each year, essential for players of American mah jongg. Other organizations publish their own cards and also function as arbiters and referees of any questions and disputes which may arise.

❧ The Symbols of the Set ❧

Part of the fascination of mah jongg lies in the mah jongg set and the images engraved on the tiles. It is no surprise that the mah jongg tiles, coming from China, are rife with symbolism. Each tile in the set reflects some universal aspect of human nature, seen through the prism of Chinese life and culture. Let's examine a few.

In mah jongg, there are groups of tiles called Suits. In American mah jongg, one of the Suits is called Bams, representing the bamboo plant. The tiles are stamped with little bamboo twigs. Bamboo is the most versatile plant in China, used for building, food, writing implements, clothing, furniture, and a myriad of other things, including mah jongg tiles. Because bamboo is so important in Chinese life and culture, it's represented in the set and is symbolic of strength, service, versatility, and usefulness.

Interestingly, the first tile of the Bam Suit is stamped with an image not of a bamboo twig, but of a bird, usually a peacock. In some older sets, the birds are sometimes shown soaring; there are also "sparrow" sets, in which the bird is perched on a bamboo stalk. These "sparrow" sets can be seen as a reference to the name *mah jongg,* sometimes interpreted as "The Game of Sparrows."

Birds are emblems of beauty and grace, but to some, the image of the peacock is seen as preening. Therefore, the peacock tile has been interpreted to mean vanity, or a love of one's own image.

Another Suit in American mah jongg is called Crak. In Chinese, this Suit is called Wan, which literally means "the 10,000s." In Chinese, when you refer to *wan*, it's like saying something is universal, that it's everywhere. The universal character values of truth, kindness, loyalty, fidelity, honor, etc., existing in all societies, are so highly esteemed in the Chinese culture that they have been symbolically put into the mah jongg set. In English, the Crak Suit has come to be known as the Character Suit, paying homage to the values of *wan*.

A third Suit in American mah jongg is called Dot; in the Chinese game it is called Circles. These tiles are stamped to look like balls or dots and they are associated with coins or money. The first tile of this Suit is interpreted to be a precious and valuable pearl. So the Dot Suit symbolizes wealth and luxury, and because of its connection to coins or money, it is also symbolic of business or commerce.

The set also contains tiles called Flowers. They depict images of a plum blossom, an orchid, a chrysanthemum and of course, bamboo—plants that are symbolic of death, life, fertility, heaven and earth, and so on. In Chinese mah jongg, the Flower tiles are also associated with the seasons—the delicate plum blossom with spring, the exotic orchid with summer, the beautiful chrysanthemum with fall and the sturdy, hardy bamboo with winter. In some very old sets the Flower tiles are stamped with pictures of mandarins, symbolic of the elite class. More modern sets have images of simple, ordinary people who are engaged in ordinary tasks—teachers, farmers, fishermen, scribes, etc. Though "ordinary," these people are honored via tiles in Chinese mah jongg. These tiles are worth more in scoring—perhaps a metaphor for a belief in the high worth and value due to every one of us, regardless of our station in life.

Every tile in the mah jongg set has its own symbolism, reflecting the culture, ideals, and spiritual values of a world in which we all participate. These few examples give you an idea of the serious matters the tiles represent. So when you play mah jongg, remember, you are not just playing with arbitrary tiles, but with many symbolic metaphors of life.

Now, a big warm *welcome!* We're off to a challenging, exciting adventure in the world of American mah jongg!

Let's turn our attention to these "metaphors of life," the first stop on our voyage.

ༀ CHAPTER 2 ༀ
Unraveling the Mystery of the Tiles

When you make your first Mah Jongg, your heart races, your palms sweat, you breathe fast, and your stomach churns. The thrill of victory! A winning smile from ear to ear! It's a great feeling.

I know you are anxious to play and I don't blame you. And I know you have many questions. How do you get tiles? Do other players see your tiles? How do you play? How do you make combinations? These are all great questions and if I answered, "You get your tiles from the Wall," you'd ask "What's the Wall?"

In order to understand the answers to your questions, you need to first understand the basics of the game—the tiles, how to interpret the Card of Hands, why it is important in the game, how to start a hand, how to select a hand from the card, how to do the Charleston (the *what?*) and then after all that, how to put everything together to actually play the game and win! As we go from chapter to chapter you will see that the answers to all your questions will be revealed. So let's put them aside for now and turn our attention to the first fundamental you need to understand the game. There is a summary and a quiz at the end of this chapter that will help you with the material you've just learned.

One more word. You will need a set, in order to practice and to play. The modern American mah jongg set comes with 152 tiles, four racks, dice and betting chips. The chips are used in the Chinese game for betting, but most players of American mah jongg don't use them. Many people have inherited older sets from friends or relatives or have acquired older sets elsewhere. Sets made before 1961 do not contain Joker tiles (see "Jokers," below). To be useful for American mah jongg, sets must contain eight Jokers. Consult the Appendix for more information about how to make your older set useable for American mah jongg. Chinese and Japanese sets are not suitable for playing American mah jongg because they contain only 144 tiles and do not include the necessary racks to hold the tiles, nor do they include Joker tiles.

Let's begin by focusing on the tiles, their functions, and their uses in the game.

In American mah jongg there are five different categories of tiles: Suit tiles, Dragon tiles, Wind tiles, Flower tiles, and Joker tiles—152 tiles in all.

✎ Suits ✎

The first group of tiles is called **Suits**.

Mah jongg has three **Suits**: **Dots**, **Bams** and **Craks**. Each Suit has tiles numbered 1 through 9. There are four tiles of each number, for a total of 36 tiles in each Suit. All together, there are 108 Suit tiles: 4 x 9 = 36 tiles per Suit, x 3 Suits = 108.

DOTS

The first Suit is called **Dot**. These are easy to identify because they are images of dots, or circles, or balls. Each Dot tile has a number stamped in the upper left-hand corner, indicating the number of dots on the tile. There is one dot on the 1-Dot, two dots on the 2-Dot and so on, up to 9-Dot. There are four tiles of each numeral—totaling 36 tiles in all.

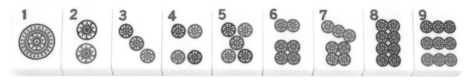

Dots

 DO IT Find one set of Dots (1–9) and place them in front of you.

BAMS

The next Suit is called **Bam** (short for bamboo). This Suit is also easy to distinguish because the tiles are predominately green and the images represent bamboo twigs. Like the Dots, these tiles also have numbers stamped in the upper left-hand corner, from 1 to 9, and there are four tiles of each numeral, 36 in all.

But in this Suit, the *1-Bam tile is an image of a bird,* not an image of bamboo twigs. It is usually some design variation of a peacock or a crane. In some older sets, the image might be a soaring bird or a sparrow perched on a bamboo stalk. It's important to recognize that the 1-Bam tile is totally different from the rest of the Bam Suit, as you can see here:

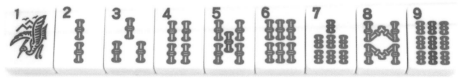

Bams

1-Bams

Make some kind of association with the 1-Bam and a bird that will help you remember the 1-Bam tile.

 DO IT　Find one set of Bams (1–9) and place them next to the Dot Suit.

CRAKS

The third Suit is called **Crak**. It is distinguished by a red Chinese character (which means *wan*; see page 19) stamped on the bottom half of the tile. You will find the numbers, 1 to 9, stamped on the top part of these tiles as well. Also, on the top half of the tile is the Chinese character for the number that each tile represents. As with the Dots and Bams, there are four tiles of each number, 36 in all.

Craks

 DO IT　Place one set of Craks (1–9) in front of you, next the Dots and Bams.

That takes care of the three **Suits**: **Dots**, **Bams**, and **Craks**.

❦ Dragons ❧

The next category of tiles is called **Dragons**. There are three groups of Dragons: **Red Dragons**, **Green Dragons** and **Soap Dragons**. They are stamped with a dragon-like figure, but often, in older sets, Chinese characters are used to represent the Dragons. Again, there are four tiles of each Dragon, 12 in all.

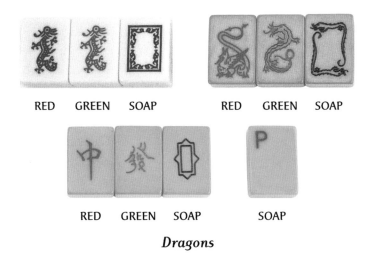

RED   GREEN   SOAP   RED   GREEN   SOAP

RED   GREEN   SOAP   SOAP

Dragons

The Red Dragon is red and it is called **Red**.

The Green Dragon is green, called **Green**.

The third Dragon used to be called White, because it was a blank tile, symbolically representing the unknown. In some older sets from the 1930s, Whites had a "P" for *po*, which means white in Chinese, engraved in the upper left-hand corner. It is still a mostly blank tile but now has a small blue border. Today, in American mah jongg, this Dragon is called **Soap**. (Why? Research hasn't turned up a definitive answer.) It might be easier to remember if you think of it as a bar of soap.

MATCHING DRAGONS

Even though Dragon tiles are a distinct entity, each Dragon is associated with or matches a different Suit. This phenomenon is called **matching Dragon**. The

CRAK MATCHES RED   **BAM MATCHES GREEN**   **DOT MATCHES SOAP**
A CRAK/RED DRAGON   A BAM/GREEN DRAGON   A DOT/SOAP DRAGON

Matching Dragons

Red Dragon matches **Crak** because of the red symbol on the bottom half of the tile. The **Green Dragon** matches **Bam** because the Bam tiles are predominately green. And the **Soap Dragon**, by process of elimination, matches **Dot**.

 Now place a Dragon next to its matching Suit.

> *Hint:* It can be easier to remember this concept by thinking of the Suits and Dragons as color-coded; **Red/Crak, Green/Bam** and **Soap/Dot**.

SOAP ALSO REPRESENTS A ZERO

Besides being a Dragon that matches Dot, *Soap has another function. It is used as a "0."* Certain combinations on the Card of Hands (see next chapter) require zeros, such as the year 2004 on the sample card we'll be using. There are no other tiles that represent "0," so when a zero is required, you must use the Soap Dragon. *It then becomes **neutral**.* This means Soap can be used as a "0" not only with its matching Dot Suit, but with any other Suit. See the examples below.

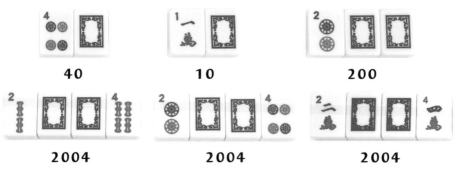

40   10   200

2004   2004   2004

Soaps used as "0"s

So Soap has a dual function: it is a Dragon and also a *neutral* "0."

There are other neutral tiles that will be introduced as we go along. *Any neutral tile* may be used with any other tile in the set.

☙ Winds ❧

The next group of tiles is called **Winds**: North, South, East, and West. Easy to identify, they are marked with the initials N, S, E, W. There are four tiles of each Wind, for a total of 16. *Winds are also **neutral** tiles.*

Winds

 DO IT Find one set of Wind tiles and place them next to your other tiles.

☙ Flowers ❧

The next group of tiles is called **Flowers**. They are the most artistic and creatively designed of all the tiles and very distinctive. The flowers represented are plum blossom, chrysanthemum, orchid and, of course, bamboo, the most versatile plant in China. In older sets, as well as modern sets, the images of Flower tiles may vary from one set to another. All the flowers represented carry weighty symbolism in Chinese culture.

There are eight Flower tiles, usually four tiles representing flowers and four tiles representing people. It doesn't matter if the images are of flowers or of people. They are all part of the Flower family, and called Flower. All modern American sets include both types, but people tiles are not found in some older sets. These sets only have images of flowers. Sometimes, Flower tiles are stamped with the seasons and/or numbers. In the American mah jongg game these markings have no relevance so don't pay attention to them. *Flowers are neutral*.

Flowers

 DO IT Select a couple of Flower tiles and place them with the other tiles.

❧ Jokers ☙

And finally, the last tiles are the **Jokers**. Easily distinguished, they are stamped with the word "Joker." Jokers are like wild cards, and are very useful because they can replace any or all tiles in certain combinations needed for a hand. *Jokers are also* **neutral**, like the Winds, Flowers and Soap (when used as a "0"). There are eight Jokers.

Jokers

 DO IT Put a couple of Jokers next to the other tiles.

Next, we will learn how to use these tiles to make the proper combinations needed for a hand. *Combinations are made by grouping* **matching tiles** *together*.

Matching tiles are identical tiles of the same Suit and same number, or same Dragon, same Wind, or same Flower. Two matching tiles are a **Pair**, three matching tiles are a **Pung**, four matching tiles are a **Kong**, five matching tiles are a **Quint**, and six matching tiles are a **Sextet**. In card games, this is referred to as "two of a kind," "three of a kind," "four of a kind," and so on. But in mah jongg, it is referred to as matching tiles. These combinations are the basic building blocks of all hands and are going to be part of every mah jongg hand you play. The pictures below are examples of matching tiles.

2 2 BAM	**4 4 4** CRAK	**D D D D** GREEN
Pair (two matching tiles)	**Pung** (three matching tiles)	**Kong** (four matching tiles)

N N N N J NORTH	**F F F F F F** FLOWER
Quint (five matching tiles). Requires at least one Joker (except in a Quint of Flowers).	**Sextet** (six matching tiles). Requires at least two Jokers (except in a Sextet of Flowers).

Matching Tiles

Study these examples carefully, then do the following:

Put the necessary tiles together for:

1. A **Pair** of Red Dragons
2. A **Kong** of Flowers
3. A **Pung** of East
4. A **Quint** of 3-Craks
5. A **Kong** of 1-Bams
6. A **Pair** of 7-Craks
7. A **Pung** of 2-Dots
8. A **Sextet** of any matching tiles

Check your answers:

1. **D D**
2. **F F F F**
3. **E E E**
4. **3 3 3 3 J**
5. **1 1 1 1**
6. **7 7**
7. **2 2 2**
8. **F F F F F F** or your choice of tile.

Jokers can only be used in the following combinations: a **Pung**, a **Kong**, a **Quint**, or a **Sextet**.

Jokers may replace any tiles *only* in a Pung, Kong, Quint or Sextet. You may use as many Jokers as you wish (or have) for these combinations. Additionally, you are allowed to create combinations using *all* Jokers as well. When you use all Jokers, you do not need an identifying tile, which is a tile that identifies the combination.

What about **Pairs**? *You may not use any Jokers in a Pair or for a Single tile. Never!*

The following examples illustrate possible combinations of Jokers and tiles for a Pung, Kong, Quint and Sextet.

Example: Matching Tiles Using Jokers

Pung of 8-Bam	**Kong of 2-Dot**	**Quint of 7-Crak**
a. **8 8 J** (1 Joker)	a. **2 2 2 J** (1 Joker)	a. **7 7 7 7 J** (1 Joker)
b. **8 J J** (2 Jokers)	b. **2 2 J J** (2 Jokers)	b. **7 7 7 J J** (2 Jokers)
c. **J J J** (3 Jokers)	c. **2 J J J** (3 Jokers)	c. **7 7 J J J** (3 Jokers)
	d. **J J J J** (4 Jokers)	d. **7 J J J J** (4 Jokers)
		e. **J J J J J** (5 Jokers)

Sextet of various tiles

a. **F F F F F F** (No Jokers) Flower

b. **1 1 1 1 J J** (2 Jokers) 1-Crak

c. 2 2 2 **J J J** (3 Jokers) 2-Bam

d. **D D J J J J** (4 Jokers) Soap

e. **3 J J J J J** (5 Jokers) 3-Dot

f. **J J J J J J** (6 Jokers) 4-Crak

Study these examples carefully and then do the following:

Put the necessary tiles together, using Jokers, for:

1. A **Pung** of Flowers (use 2 Jokers)
2. A **Kong** of Souths (use 3 Jokers)
3. A **Quint** of 2-Craks (use 2 Jokers)
4. A **Kong** of Green Dragons (use all Jokers)
5. A **Sextet** of 9-Bams (use 3 Jokers)
6. A **Pung** of 5-Dots (use all Jokers)
7. A **Pung** of 6-Craks (use 1 Joker)

Check your answers:

1. **F J J**
2. **S J J J**
3. **2 2 2 J J**
4. **J J J J**
5. **9 9 9 J J J**
6. **J J J**
7. **6 6 J**

❧ Discarding Tiles ❧

When you discard a tile, you must place it face up in the center of the table, and correctly announce it, identifying it by its Suit and number or name. For example, say "4-Crak," "9-Dot," "8-Bam," "Flower" (no number or Season, please). Winds are identified by their direction, simply "North," "South," "East," or "West." For the Dragons, say "Red," "Soap," or "Green." If and when you discard a Joker, you may say "Same" to indicate the previously discarded tile, or you may say "Joker." Either is acceptable.

Now you have learned the names of the tiles, and you can identify them, their functions, and the concept of matching Dragons. You know what matching tiles are—the combinations of Pairs, Pungs, Kongs, Quints and Sextets—and you know how to use Jokers in these combinations. Great!

We have covered a lot of information and I realize there are so many new things you need to remember. You may want to reread this chapter to solidify your understanding of the information. Here is a summary of the important information for you to study and use to refresh your memory. The quiz that follows can help you make sure you understand all the ideas in this chapter before you go on to the next.

Chapter 2 Summary

⬤ The Tiles

• **3 Suits**—*Bams, Dots, Craks:* 1–9, 4 of each number	108
• **4 Winds**—*North, South, East, West:* 4 of each	16
• **3 Dragons**—*Red, Green, Soap:* 4 of each	12
• **Flowers**	8
• **Jokers**	8
	Total: 152

    • 1-Bam is an image of a bird.

⊛ Suits and their matching Dragons:
- **Bam** matches **Green**
- **Dot** matches **Soap**
- **Crak** matches **Red**

⊛ Neutral tiles can be used with any tile.
- Soap—when used as a "0"
- Flowers
- Jokers
- Winds

⊛ Matching tiles are tiles of the same Suit and number, same Dragon, same Wind or Flower.
- **Pair**—2 matching tiles (No Jokers)
- **Pung**—3 matching tiles (Use up to three Jokers)
- **Kong**—4 matching tiles (Use up to four Jokers)
- **Quint**—5 matching tiles (Use up to five Jokers)
- **Sextet**—6 matching tiles (Use up to six Jokers)

⊛ Jokers can substitute for any or all tiles in a Pung, Kong, Quint or Sextet.

⊛ Never use a Joker in a Pair or for a Single tile.

⊛ An identifying tile is not needed when all Jokers are used.

⊛ When you discard a tile, identify it by Suit and number, Dragon color, Wind direction, or as a Flower or Joker.

Let's now turn our attention to the next phase of the basics of the game. In the next chapter, we are going to learn to unlock the mysteries of the mah jongg card. Like Sherlock Holmes, we are going to "Crack the Code."

❧ QUIZ ❧

Unraveling the Mystery of the Tiles

1. What are the three Suits?

2. Which Dragons match which Suits?

3. How many Flower tiles are there?

4. The Soap tile is a Dragon. What is the other use for the Soap?

5. Explain neutral tiles. Which tiles are neutral?

6. How many total Dot tiles are there? How many total Dragons?

7. Which tile shows an image of a bird?

8. In what combinations can Jokers be used?

9. How many Wind tiles are there?

10. What are matching tiles?

11. How many Jokers can you use in a Pair? Pung? Kong?

12. Do you need an identifying tile when you use all Jokers in a combination?

ANSWERS

1. Bams, Dots, Craks.
2. Green matches Bams.
   Red matches Craks.
   Soap matches Dots.
3. 8.
4. Soap is also used as "0."
5. A neutral tile can be used with any tile in the set. Neutral tiles are Winds, Flowers, Jokers and Soap, only when it is used as a "0."
6. 36, 12.

7. 1-Bam.
8. Jokers may be used in a Pung, Kong, Quint or Sextet.
9. 16.
10. Matching tiles are tiles of the same Suit and number, same Dragon, same Wind or Flower. A Pair, Pung, Kong, Quint and Sextet are matching tiles.
11. None. Up to three. Up to four.
12. No.

❧ CHAPTER 3 ❧

Cracking the Code

A card, a card! My kingdom for a card! Well, maybe you wouldn't trade your kingdom, but you need a mah jongg card. Why? Because in American mah jongg you cannot create your own hands, only the hands specified on a card are acceptable. The hand a player completes must correspond to a hand on a card. The player who is the first to assemble the correct combinations of tiles needed to match one of these hands, wins.

The card is made up of nine or ten different categories, each requiring a specific kind of tile. Within each category there are several individual hands, for a total of about 50 to 55 hands on any card. Each hand designates the specific combinations of tiles needed to complete it. New cards are published each year, usually containing the same categories, but within these categories the individual hands vary. Because the hands change annually, you will want to get a new card each year to keep current.

For purposes of learning, we will be referring to the standard card, called the "Official Standard Hands and Rules," published by the National Mah Jongg League (NMJL). With generous permission from the NMJL, the card published for the year 2004 is reproduced in the back of the book for your use. It makes no difference in what year the card is printed, because the principles to understand it remain the same.

QUINTS

	VALUES
22 333 4444 55555 (These Nos. Only)	x 40
NNNNN DDDD 11111 (Quint Any Wind & Arty No. In Any Suit–Kong Any Dragon)	x 45
FF 22222 33 444411 (Any 3 Consecutive Nos., Any 3 Suits)	x 45
FF 11111 + 99999 = 10 (Any 3 Suits)	x 45

CONSECUTIVE RUN

	VALUES
11 222 3333 444 55 or 55 666 7777 888 99 (Any 4 Consecutive Nos., Any 2 Suits)	x 25
111 2222 333 4444 (Any 4 Consecutive Nos., Any 2 Suits)	x 25
111 22 222 3333 (Any 3 Consecutive Nos., Any 3 Suits)	x 25
FFFF 1111 2222 DD (Any 2 Consecutive Nos.)	x 25
11 22 333 4444 5555 (Any 5 Consecutive Pairs, Kongs Ascending Nos. Any 3 Suits)	x 30
222 44 6666 88 88 (Any 3 Suits Pairs 8's Only)	c 35

13579

	VALUES
11 333 5555 777 99	x 25
1111 3333 333 5555 or 555 7777 777 9999 (Any 2 Suits)	x 25
11 33 555 777 9999 (Any 3 Suits)	x 30
FF 5555 77 9999 DD	x 30
5555 77 9999 DD	x 30
11 33 11 33 55 1111 (Any 3 Suits, Kong 1, 3 or 5)	x 25
55 77 55 77 99 99 (Any 3 Suits, 5, 6 or 9)	x 30
FFFF 3333 x 5555 = 15 or FFFF 5555 x 7777 = 35	x 30

WINDS – DRAGONS

	VALUES
FFF NN EE WWW SSSS (Pairs Any Like Odd Nos.)	x 25
NNNN 11 1111 SSSS (Pairs Any Like Even Nos.)	x 30
EEEE 22 22 22 WWWW (Pair Any Dragon)	x 30
NN DD 222 DDD DDDD (Pair Any Wind)	x 30
EE DD WWW DDD DDDD (Pair Any Dragon)	x 25
NNNN EEEE WWWW SS (Pair Any 2 Suits)	x 30

369

	VALUES
FF 33 66 999 DDDD	x 25
FF 3333 6666 9999 (Any 3 Suits)	x 25
333 66 999 333 333 (Any 2 Suits, Like Pungs 3, 6 or 9)	x 30
33 666 DDDD 666 99 (Any 3 Suits)	x 30
33 66 333 666 9999 (Any 3 Suits, Kong 9's Only)	x 25
FF 3 66 999 3 66 9999 (Any 2 Suits)	x 30

SINGLES AND PAIRS

	VALUES
NN EE WW SS 11 22 33 (Any 3 Consecutive Nos.)	x 45
FF 11 DD 11 44 55 DD (Any 5 Consecutive Nos.)	c 50
FF 11 DD 11 DD 11 DD (3 Suits Any Like Nos.)	c 50
FF 11 22 44 66 88 99 (Any 2 Suits)	c 50
FF 3669 3669 3669	c 50
FF 2004 NEWS 2004 (1 or 2 Suits, 2 and 4 Some Suit)	c 75

NOTE: WHITE DRAGON IS USED AS ZERO "0". IT MAY BE USED WITH ANY SUIT. (CRAKS, BAMS OR DOTS)

2004

	VALUES
FF NEWS FFF 2004 (Any 2 and 4 Some Suit)	x 25
FF G·G·G·G 2004 RRRR (Kong Green & Red Dragon only, Any 2 & 4 Some Suit)	x 30
NNNN E W SSSS 2004 (Any 2 and 4 Suits)	x 30

2468

	VALUES
FF 2222 44 66 8888 or FF 2222 44 66 8888	x 25
22 44 444 666 8888 8888 (Kong 8's Only)	x 25
222 4444 666 6666 88 88 (Any 2 Suits)	x 25
2222 DDDD 888 DDDD (Any 2 Suits)	x 30
2222 44 6666 88 88 (Any 3 Suits Pairs 8's Only)	x 30
222 444 6666 888 DD	x 35

LIKE NUMBERS

	VALUES
FF 1111 1111 1111 (Any Like Nos.)	x 25
FFFF 11 111 1111 (Any Like Nos.)	x 25

ADDITION HANDS

	VALUES
FFFF 2222 + 9999 = 11 or FFFF 2222 + 9999 = 11	x 25
FFFF 3333 + 8888 = 11 or FFFF 3333 + 8888 = 11	x 25
FFFF 4444 + 7777 = 11 or FFFF 4444 + 7777 = 11	x 25

This document is protected by copyright laws. It is illegal to reproduce it.

PLAYERS SHOULD NOT THROW IN HANDS UNTIL MAH JONGG IS VERIFIED.

MISCALLED TILE: A tile cannot be claimed until correctly named. Correctly named tiles may then be called for an Exposure or Mah Jongg. HOWEVER, if Mah Jongg is called with the incorrectly named tile, the game ceases. Then, miscaller pays claimant four times the value of the hand. Others do not pay.

BONUS: WHEN A PLAYER DECLARES MAH JONGG AND NO JOKERS ARE PART OF THE HAND, A BONUS IS GIVEN. DOUBLE VALUE: EXCHANGED JOKERS FROM AN EXPOSURE CAN MAKE THE HAND JOKERLESS.

A hand is dead when it has too few or too many tiles during play or an incorrect number of exposed tiles. Dead hand ceases to pick and discard and cannot call for anything.

At no time may a tile be called to complete a pair including flower for Mah Jongg or Mah Jongg in an Exposed or Concealed Hand.

A discarded Flower may be claimed to complete a Pung or Kong or Quint of Flowers for Mah Jongg or Mah Jongg in a Concealed Hand.

Player is permitted to discard a Flower at any time during the game and call it "Flower".

RULES FOR BETTORS: Bettor pays or receives same as player bet on.

MAH JONGG IN ERROR

1. If a player declares Mah Jongg in error and does not expose the hand and all other hands are intact, play continues without penalty.
2. If a player declares Mah Jongg in error and exposes part or all of the hand and all other hands are intact, game continues but declarer's hand is dead. The same penalty applies for calling a discard or making an incorrect exposure. DEAD HAND DISCONTINUES PLAYING; DOES NOT PICK OR DISCARD. Plays winner full value of hand.
3. If a player declares Mah Jongg in error and one other player exposes part or all of the hand, the game continues with the two players whose hands are intact. If winner turns over a joker after winning, declarer exposes part or all of the hand, game cannot continue. Erring declarer pays double the value of the incorrect hand to the one player whose hand is intact.

When settling for any information, please send a stamped self-addressed envelope to:

NATIONAL MAH JONGG LEAGUE, INC. 250 West 57th Street, New York, N.Y. 10107
(212) 246-3052 FAX (212) 248-4117 www.nmjl.org
Become a Member: $6.00 includes Score Card & Bulletin
Printed in the USA

When a player Mah Jonggs on a discarded tile, DISCARDER pays the winner double value. All other players pay single value. When a player picks OWN Mah Jongg tile, all players pay double value.

BONUS: WHEN A PLAYER DECLARES MAH JONGG AND NO JOKERS ARE PART OF THE HAND, A BONUS IS GIVEN. DOUBLE VALUE: EXCHANGED JOKERS FROM AN EXPOSURE CAN MAKE THE HAND JOKERLESS.

EXCEPTION: SINGLES & PAIRS GROUP–NO JOKERS.

Run–means consecutive numbers. Pair–2 like tiles. Pung–3, Kong–4, Quint–5. 1 color–any 1 suit. 2 colors–any 2 suits. 3 colors–3 suits. F–Flower, X–Exposed, C–Concealed. D–Dragons: R–Red D; Wh–White D; G–Green D. Matching Dragons: Craks with Reds, Dots with Whites, Bams with Greens.

Note: White Dragon is used also as ZERO "0". It can be USED with any suit (Craks, Bams or Dots).

ALL TILES FACED DOWN AND MIXED. EAST ROLLS DICE and total number thrown designates where East breaks wall. East player picks 4 tiles for 3 rounds. East then picks next and 2nd top tiles and other players one tile each.

CHARLESTON (Flowers May Be Passed) Dazee Aer Plus Lecutorez Countez Bun Jokers Mar Neva Be Passez)
First Charleston compulsory–three passes (right, across, left).
Second Charleston optional–three passes (left, across, right).
Blind pass of 1, 2, or 3 tiles permitted on last pass of either Charleston, without looking at them.
Courtesy pass–optional "0". 1, 2 or 3 tiles–with player opposite, whether one or two Charlestons are played. Charleston is completed. East starts play by discarding 14th tile. Players on the right of East pick and discard in rotation. Jokers may be discarded at any time during the game and named the same as previous discard. Jokers may be exchanged to replace any tiles in any Pung, Kong, or Quint only. Joker or token may be exposed in any exposure with the like tiles by any player, whether picked from wall or on player's hand, when it is player's turn. Joker or Jokers can NEVER be used for a single tile, or in a pair.

1. NO PASSING AHEAD.
2. When two players want the same discard, one payer for an Exposure and another for Mah Jongg, Mah Jongg declarer always has preference.
3. When two players want the same tile for exposure, player next in turn to discarder has preference.
4. When two players want the same tile for Mah Jongg, player next in turn has preference.
5. A tile may not be claimed for Exposure or Mah Jongg after player next in turn has picked and racked or discarded a tile.

*The front and back of the NMJL Card of Hands for 2004.
See the back of the book for a larger copy of the card, which you may cut out
and use for reference as you work through this book.*

The card is written in a kind of code or shorthand describing which kinds of tiles and which combinations each hand requires. Before you can play, it's necessary to learn how to read this shorthand or "crack the code," because you need to translate what's printed on the card into the combinations of tiles needed for a hand.

Along with learning to crack the code, *you need to become familiar with the individual hands of the card you are using. This is the key to winning in mah jongg!* Almost every aspect of the game—choosing a hand, playing your hand, changing your hand, and using strategies—assumes a knowledge and understanding of the hands on the card. Once you master the card and its hands, you're well on your way to becoming a master (or mistress) of the game. This chapter will show you how.

At first glance, the card looks daunting. What a crazy mishmash of colors, numbers, and letters! But don't despair! There is method to this madness. We are going to unravel this jumble by separating the card into its individual elements, in order to discover what each means and how it will determine your hand. Once you crack the code, it becomes understandable and logical.

There are four elements of the card we will discuss: **Numbers, abbreviations, Sections and colors**.

Let's look at the card. The first thing you notice is rows of numbers, letters, and colors. Each row represents a different hand you can play and each hand has a different combination of numbers, letters, and colors. Also notice that the hands are divided into separate groups I call Sections. And it all looks like it's in Technicolor. What does all this mean? It's simple.

☙ Numbers ☙

The numbers correspond to the numbers on the Suit tiles, 1 through 9.

❧ Abbreviations ❧

In some hands you will also see letters. These abbreviations are for certain kinds of tiles. **D** stands for Dragons, **F** stands for Flower, and **N, E, W, S** stand for the Winds: North, East, West and South. **X** stands for Exposed hands, **C** stands for Concealed hands (see page 46). There are other abbreviations on the card that will be explained later.

❧ Sections ❧

Notice on the card there are groups of hands or Sections, each with a heading printed in bold type, such as **2468** or **Consecutive Run** or **Winds-Dragons**. These headings, which I call the theme, describe the kinds of tiles needed for a mah jongg hand. Within each Section there are several hands and each one is some variation of the Section's theme. In most Sections, besides the theme, some hands may also require Flower and Dragon tiles. In addition, since the card changes annually, Sections may be added or deleted. The most common ones are listed below.

Follow along with the card and we'll discover the theme of each Section. Starting at the far right side, they are:

Winds-Dragons requires combinations of Wind tiles and Dragon tiles. Sometimes there are Suit and number requirements as well.

369 requires various combinations of the numbers 3, 6, and 9.

Singles and Pairs requires all the hands to be made up of Pairs and/or combinations of Single tiles. No Jokers are allowed because you can't use Jokers to complete a Pair or for a Single tile. (Remember?)

Quints have hands that call for at least one combination that uses five matching tiles. In this Section, because there are only 4 of each tile, you need at least 1 Joker.

Consecutive Run requires combinations of ascending consecutively numbered tiles. The 1s, 2s, 3s, 4s, 5s printed on the card do not mean that you must only use 1s, 2s, 3s, 4s, 5s. It means that the hands require *any* ascending consecutive numbers. For example, you may use 3s, 4s, 5s, 6s or 6s, 7s, 8s, 9s for your ascending consecutive numbers. (Except in the 1st hand. This hand [1–5 or 5–9] does not allow choice of any other numbers.)

13579 designates specific combinations of *odd* numbered tiles.

2004 requires tiles that designate the current year (this card is for 2004) and some combination of Flowers, Winds, and Dragons. This Section is sometimes called Year Hands.

2468 calls for different combinations of *even* numbered tiles.

Like Numbers requires specific combinations of tiles whose numbers are all alike. For example, all 5s, all 7s, all 6s and so on. This Section is not found on all cards.

Addition or **Multiplication Hands** require designated combinations of number tiles that add up. For example: Fs, 9s + 2s =11. You need Flowers, 9s, 2s and two 1s. Don't pay attention to the "=," "+," or "x" signs. Just pay attention to the Suits and numbers. This Section is not found on all cards.

Now you know that Sections of the card designate what kind of tiles and how many of each is required to complete the hand. In *most* Sections you must follow these specifics exactly—including the numbers on the tiles. There is no variation. But there are some Sections that allow the player the choice of numbers. First, let's turn to Sections that do not allow a choice.

SECTIONS THAT DO NOT ALLOW CHOICE

- **Winds-Dragons**
- 369
- Some **Quints**
- 13579
- 2468
- 1st hand in **Consecutive Run**
- Some hands in **Singles and Pairs**

- **Addition** or **Multiplication**
- **2004** (or the current Year)

In these Sections, you must follow exactly the specifics printed for each hand. You cannot choose any Winds, numbers, or Dragons you wish, or the amount required for each combination. If the hand specifies 333 66 999, you must have three 3s (a Pung), two 6s (a Pair), three 9s (a Pung). If it specifies 555 7777 9999 you must have a Pung of 5s, a Kong of 7s, and a Kong of 9s. If the hand requires a Kong of Flowers, you must have four Flowers. If the hand calls for a Pair of Dragons, you must have two Dragons. If three Ws are required, you must have three Wests.

Note: the Consecutive Run Section allows you to choose any consecutive numbers you want, as long as they are ascending. There is one exception. The first hand of the Consecutive Run Section does not allow this choice. You must use the numbers indicated: **1 to 5** or **5 to 9**.

Now, let's examine which Sections allow a choice.

Hands in these Sections allow the player to choose the numbers on the tiles. But you cannot change the combinations, Pairs, Pungs, and Kongs, that are required.

SECTIONS THAT ALLOW CHOICE

- Most hands in **Consecutive Run**
- **Like Numbers**
- Some hands in **Quints**
- Some hands in **Singles and Pairs**

Consecutive Run Section. As noted above, all these hands (except the first one) require *any ascending consecutive numbers of your choice.* The hands are printed with 1s, 2s, 3s, 4s, and 5s to indicate only that the hands require *ascending consecutive* numbers.

You are allowed to choose any ascending consecutive numbers you wish. But, for example, if the hand calls for "Any Four Consecutive Numbers," you can't use 4s, 5s, 8s, and 9s as they are not ascending consecutive numbers. You must use 4s, 5s, 6s, and 7s or 6s, 7s, 8s, and 9s. The Consecutive Run Section can be confusing, so study the examples below very carefully.

Example:

The Card	Your Tiles
1 1 1 2 2 3 3 3 3 4 4 4 5 5 (or 5–9)	1 1 1 2 2 3 3 3 3 4 4 4 5 5 (or 5–9)
1 1 1 2 2 2 3 3 3 4 4 4	5 5 5 6 6 6 7 7 7 8 8 8
1 1 2 2 2 2 3 3 3 3 3 3 3 3	2 2 3 3 3 3 4 4 4 4 4 4 4 4
1 1 2 2 1 1 1 2 2 2 3 3 3 3	4 4 5 5 4 4 4 5 5 5 6 6 6 6
F F F F 1 1 1 1 2 2 2 2 D D	F F F F 8 8 8 8 9 9 9 9 D D

As you can see, in this Section (or in any other Section) there is never a run of single numbers that make a combination, such as 1234 or 5678. There is always some repetition of numbers.

Like Numbers Section. The card might read **11 111 1111,** but the player chooses what numbers to use, as long as they are all alike.

Example:

66 666 6666 or **99 999 9999** or **44 444 4444**

Quints Section, Singles and Pairs Section. These hands vary. They call for combinations of Single tiles and Pairs, Like tiles, Consecutive Runs, and "Any" tiles.

❧ Colors ☙

Now look again at the individual hands and you can see they are printed in colors: blue, green, and red. Each hand is printed in one, two, or three colors. The colors represent Suits.

Later on, when you look for a hand to play, the first thing you want to do is determine how many Suits (and Dragons) you need for that hand. It's easy. Count the colors. *The number of colors determines the number of Suits required for a hand.*

Hands printed in *one color mean one Suit is required* to complete the hand. Hands printed in *two colors mean two Suits are required* to complete the hand. Hands printed in *three colors mean all three Suits are required.*

 Look at the 2004 NMJL card and find several hands with one, two, and three colors that reflect one, two, and three Suits.

Since the colors on the card are blue, red and green, you might assume that the color corresponds to a specific Suit (or Dragon). Does blue mean you must use Dots, red mean you must use Craks and green mean you must use Bams? *No!* Although the different colors are a simple way for you to determine how many Suits (and/or Dragons) are required for the hand, it does not mandate *which* Suits (or Dragons) you must use.

When one Suit is required, you may choose *any* one Suit; when you count two Suits, you choose *any* two Suits; and three Suits allow you to assemble the three Suits *in any order* you wish. *The player chooses which Suits or Dragons to use for which combinations.*

We learned that Dragons are a distinct entity and that certain Dragons match certain Suits. For purposes of determining the number of Suits a hand requires, count Dragons as if they were Suits. So *when the color of a Suit and Dragon are the same, count it as one Suit.* The term **matching Dragon**, in this instance, is used to define a Dragon that is the same color as a Suit. (See Examples 1 and 2 below.)

When the Suits and Dragons are separate colors, count the Dragons as if they were separate Suits. (See Example 3 below.)

Just a reminder: we learned that Flowers, Winds and Soaps (when used as a "0") are neutral. Neutral tiles are neither Suits nor Dragons, so *don't count them when you determine the number of Suits you need for a hand.* On the card, neutral tiles are always printed in blue.

Let's look at the examples below that reflect these ideas, as well as the concept that the colors on the card show you which Pairs, Pungs, Kongs, Quints and Sextets belong together.

These examples are not duplicates of hands on the NMJL 2004 card, but they reflect the way hands on any card are presented, in one, two, and three colors.

Examples:

1) **3 3 3 3   6 6 6   9 9 9   DDDD**
2) 4 4 4   5 5 5   6 6 6 6   **DDDD**
3) **F F**   2 2   4 4   **DDD**   6 6   **8 8 8**

The first example is all *one color,* which indicates the hand requires *any one Suit.* Since the Dragons (Ds) are the same color as the Suit, it means the matching Dragon is required.

If you choose Bams for the 3s, 6s, 9s you will then need a Kong of Green Dragons to complete the hand. If you choose Dots for the 3s, 6s, 9s, then you need a Kong of Soap Dragons. Craks would require a Kong of Red Dragons to complete the hand.

In the second example, *two colors* means the hand requires *any two Suits.* The 4s and 6s are matching colors, which means they must be in any one Suit. The 5s and Dragons (Ds) are matching colors which means they must be in any second Suit. The Dragon must match whatever Suit is chosen for the second Suit.

If you choose Craks for the 4s and 6s, Bams for the 5s, what Dragon will you need to complete the hand? Green, because the Green Dragon matches Bams. You need a Kong of Green Dragons.

In the third example, *three colors* mean that the hand requires *all three Suits*, in any order you wish. *Count the Dragons as if they were a separate Suit,* but do not count the neutral Flowers (F) as a separate Suit.

Let's say you choose Bams for the 2s and 4s for one Suit, Craks for the 6s and 8s for the second Suit. The logic here is that you use the Dragon that matches the unused third Suit. The remaining third Suit is Dots and the Dragon that matches Dots is Soap. So you would have to use a Pung of Soaps to complete the hand.

Let's look at another example: **333 6666 9999 DDD**

Again, *all three Suits are required.* The Dragons (Ds) are counted as the third Suit. You choose Dots for the 3s and 6s (one Suit), Craks for the 9s (second Suit) and the unused remaining third Suit is Bams. The matching Dragon is Green. Therefore, to complete the hand you need a Pung of Greens.

This circumstance is sometimes referred to on the card (see "Instructions," page 48) as **Opp. Dragon,** which simply means "opposite Dragon." The hand calls for the Dragon that goes with an unused remaining third Suit.

 DO IT Find several hands on the 2004 NMJL card that require matching Dragons and opposite Dragons.

Check your answers:

Matching Dragons:

> 4th and 6th hand in **2468 Section**
> 4th hand in **Consecutive Run Section**
> 4th and 5th hands in **13579 Section**
> 1st hand in **369 Section**

Opposite Dragons:

> 6th hand in **Consecutive Run Section**
>
> 4th hand in **369 Section**

The examples above demonstrate these important principles: 1) how to determine how many Suits or Dragons a hand requires, 2) the player chooses which Suits or Dragons to use to complete combinations and 3) matching colors show which combinations belong together.

Another essential principle of the card is that *when the same numbers are repeated in different colors, you must repeat those same numbers, but in a different Suit. The same is true for the Dragons.* Here are some examples.

Examples:

1) **3 3   6 6**   3 3 3   6 6 6   9 9 9 9
2) 2 2   4 4   **2 2   4 4   6 6**   8 8 8 8
3) **N N   S S   D D D   D D D   D D D D**

In the first example, the 3s and the 6s repeat. So you must have a Pair of 3s and a Pair of 6s in any one Suit (one color) and a Pung of 3s and a Pung of 6s in any second Suit (second color).

In the second example, the 2s and 4s repeat, again in different Suits. Therefore, you must have a Pair of 2s and a Pair of 4s in any one Suit and the second Pair of 2s and 4s in any second Suit.

In the third example, the hand calls for all three Dragons: Red, Green, and Soap in any order you wish. You must pay attention to which Dragons you use for the Pungs and which other Dragon you use for the Kong.

 DO IT   Find several hands on the NMJL 2004 card that have numbers or Dragons that repeat but in different colors.

Check your answers:

2nd hand in **2004 Section**
4th and 5th hands in **2468 Section**
1st and 2nd hands in **Like Numbers Section**
3rd and 6th hands in **Consecutive Run Section**
6th and 7th hands in **13579 Section**
2nd, 3rd, 4th and 5th hands in **Winds-Dragons Section**
5th and 6th hands in **369 Section**
3rd, 6th and 7th hands in **Singles and Pairs Section**

Now you know how to read the colors on the card. By using these concepts, you will be able to match your tiles to a hand on the card, which is a basic skill you need for every hand you will play.

✺ X, C, and Values ✺

Look to the right of any hand on the card and you will see some hands have an **X** next to them and some have a **C**.

*X indicates that you are playing an **Exposed** hand* and means you may "call a tile" from the discards followed by an exposure of a Pung, Kong, Quint or Sextet on top of your rack for everyone to see. Calling a tile and Exposing will be explained in Chapter 7, "The Play's the Thing."

*C indicates that you are playing a **Concealed** hand.* This means you may not call for any tile, except for the 14th tile you need for Mah Jongg. This will also be discussed more fully in Chapter 7.

The **Values** column indicates how much money each hand is worth in cents. The harder the hand is to make, the higher the monetary value. The colored chips that come with your set are a holdover from the Chinese version of the game, used for calculating points for the value of a hand. Most players use the monetary value printed on the card and disregard the chips. Of course, if you play for money, you are free to assess any value you wish to the hands.

Chapter 3 Summary of the Elements

Numbers correspond to the numbers on Suit tiles.

Abbreviations indicate Dragons, Flowers and the Winds, **N, E, W, S.**

* **X** means the hand is **Exposed**. The player is allowed to call a tile followed by an exposure of a combination.

* **C** means the hand is **Concealed** and the player is not allowed to call for any tile, except for the 14th Mah Jongg tile.

Sections tell you what kinds of tiles and how many of each tile are required to complete a hand for Mah Jongg.

* *No Choice of Tiles Allowed*

    Winds-Dragons
    369
    Some **Quints**
    13579
    2468
    1st hand in **Consecutive Run**
    Some **Singles and Pairs**
    Addition or **Multiplication**
    2004 (or current Year)

* *Choice of Tiles Allowed*

    Most hands in **Consecutive Run**
    Like Numbers
    Some hands in **Quints**
    Some hands in **Singles and Pairs**

Colors represent how many Suits and Dragons the hand requires and also reflect the tiles that belong together.

* **One color** indicates **any one Suit, and its matching Dragon.**

- • **Two colors** indicate **any two Suits and/or Dragons.**
- • **Three colors** indicate **all three Suits and/or Dragons, in any order.**

⊛ Count Dragons as if they were Suits.

- • One Suit, when the Dragon is the same color as the Suit. The dragon is a **matching Dragon.**
- • Two or more Suits, when the Dragon is a different color from the Suits.

⊛ Neutral tiles are always printed in blue. *Do not count neutral tiles.*

⊛ Matching colors indicate which combinations (Pair, Pung, Kong, Quint, Sextet) and what Suits/Dragons belong together.

⊛ Repeated numbers in different colors mean you must repeat the numbers but in different Suits.

⊛ **Values** indicate the monetary value of the hand in cents.

Wow! What a lesson! You may find it helpful to reread this section and go over parts that may have been challenging. Or if you wish, keep going, because there is still another important aspect of the card we must cover—the Instructions printed on the card next to most of the hands.

⊷ Instructions ⊶

Upon closer examination we find that there are Instructions in parentheses printed next to many hands on the card. New Instructions are printed on each new card, but just as the code remains the same, the Instructions remain basically the same as well. Once you understand them, they're easy to follow, no matter which card you are using.

In most hands, you can easily see how many Suits are required, what number tiles you need, whether you need Pairs, Pungs, or Kongs, which Dragons, and the number of Flowers. There are also hands that do not have any Instructions. In these instances, the hands need no explanation.

However, there are some hands in which the Instructions offer you options, particularly when they read "Any" or "Or". When the Instructions offer options, you need to pay attention to them. The following explanations and examples will help to clarify these Instructions.

INSTRUCTIONS THAT OFFER THE PLAYER OPTIONS

- **Any Like Odd Numbers (or Even).** This means you choose the odd or even numbers, but they must be all alike. Pay attention to the *Pairs, Pungs, or Kongs* and how many Suits are required.

  Example: Pung Like Odds   Pair Like Evens   Kong Like Evens

  555 555 555   22 22 22   4444 4444 4444

- **Any Number, Any Suit, Any Dragon,** or **Any Wind.** The player chooses *any* number, *any* Suit, *any* Dragon, *any* Wind.

- **Kong** or **Pung numbers followed by "or".** The player is free to choose *one* of the numbers indicated.

  Example: Kong (or Pung) 1, 3 *or* 5; 5, 7 *or* 9; 3, 6 *or* 9; or 2, 4, 6 *or* 8 means you choose any one number to Kong (or Pung).

- **Kong (Pung or Pair) 8s Only.** The number may change, depending on the card, so it may be an 8 or some other number.

  Example: **222   444   666   8888** (Kong 8s Only)

  33   66   99   999 (Pung 9s Only)

- In the 2004 Section, the card reading **Any 2 and 4 Same Suit** means you need a 2 and a 4 in the same Suit. Since the card changes annually, so does the designation for the year. For example, the 2006 card reads **Any 2 and 6 Same Suit.**

  Example: **2004**   **2004**

  (correct—2 and 4 match)   (incorrect—2 and 4 don't match)

  Notice here that a Pair of Soap Dragons are used for the two "0"s. Remember, Soaps are neutral when used as "0." Don't count them. No Jokers are allowed to be used in the Pair of Soaps, or for the 2 and 4 Single tiles.

Note: In the 2004 Section, in the 2nd hand **G** stands for Green Dragon and **R** stands for Red Dragon. The Instructions next to the hand clearly indicate it.

⊛ Sometimes the Instructions will read "**Opp. Dragon.**" This means Opposite Dragon. It indicates you must use the Dragon that matches the unused third Suit.

Example: **333 666 9999 DDDD**

There are hands in other Sections, such as **Singles and Pairs** and **Quints**, in which the Instructions vary for each hand. Be sure you check the Instructions for all hands.

EXAMPLES OF INSTRUCTIONS

1. **NNN EE WW SSS DDD** (Pung Any Dragon)
   Use any Dragon to complete the hand.

2. **FF 11 22 3333 4444** (Any Four Consecutive Nos., Any Two Suits)
   FF 44 55 6666 7777 *is one possible hand.*

3. **FF 222 44 66 88 88** (Pairs 8s Only)
   The hand must contain two pairs of 8s in two other Suits.

4. Any **2** and **4**, Same Suit.
   The 2 and 4 Suit must match.

5. **EEEE 11 11 11 WWWW** (Pairs Any Like Odd No.)
   Three Pairs of 1s, 3s, 5s, 7s, or 9s in 3 different Suits. (**55 55 55**) (**99 99 99**) *Or "Pairs Any Like Even No.":* *Three Pairs of 2s, 4s, 6s, or 8s, in 3 different Suits.* (**22 22 22**) (**66 66 66**)

6. **111 333 5555 5555** (Like Kongs, 1 or 3 or 5, Any Three Suits)
   Two Kongs of 1 or 3 or 5 in the two other Suits. (**111 333 1111 1111**)

7. **222 DDDD 888 DDDD** (Any Two Suits)
    Use any two Suits with their matching Dragons.

8. Pung 3, 6, or 9
    Pung of any one *number 3, 6, or 9.*

9. **2222 2222** (Kongs Any Like Even Nos.)
    Kong of 2s, 4s, 6s, or 8s.

We've spent a lot of time (and pages) learning the code and how to decipher it. But being able to decipher the card isn't enough. The essential factor is that you must become very familiar with the individual hands in each of the Sections. No, you don't have to memorize every individual hand, but *you must be conversant with what Sections require what kinds of tiles, and the combinations of different hands in the Sections. This is the key to everything else in the game.*

Why? Because you will be looking for a hand on the card to match the tiles you pick. You need to already know where the Sections are located on the card, that even numbers go with 2468 hands, that there are Winds hands that require Dragons, that you can extrapolate the numbers in the Consecutive Run Section and much more. Otherwise, you will spend your time and energy hunting for hands on the card, not knowing where to look. You will have a hard time finding a hand to play. And as you play, you won't be able to discard or defend properly, nor will you be able to change your hand, or do any of the things you need to win. Mah jongg is a fast-paced game and searching laboriously for a hand is no fun for you or anybody else. If you don't know the hands on the card, you will find playing the game tedious and you won't be a successful player. In the following chapters you will see how your knowledge of the hands on the card is crucial.

So how do you learn the hands? I strongly recommend you do the next exercise to help you. The exercise will let you experience how all the ideas we discussed so far come together. The more conscientious you are in doing this exercise, the more familiar you will become with the hands, and the more fun you will have playing mah jongg. Let me again stress the importance of knowing the hands on the card. It is the essential key to everything connected to the game.

The quiz on the following pages will also help further your understanding of the card.

I think we need a break here. So after you finish the exercise and the quiz, we'll do just that. A "Construction Project" will show us how to first build the Wall and then break it.

◢◎ EXERCISE ◎◣
Learn the Hands on the Card

This exercise will familiarize you with the card and the hands and show you what a mah jongg hand looks like.

Start with one Section of the card at a time and put the tiles together for each hand until you have done them all. As you do each hand, make a mental note of the kinds of tiles you are using and the combinations called for. For example, in the 13579 Section, you will be using odd-numbered tiles. After you have finished assembling all the hands in that Section, you will have the connection that odd tiles and the 13579 Section go together. Do the same hands in different Suits. Then move on to another Section and do the same thing—assemble the tiles required for each hand.

You will automatically begin to remember the hands you do and what Sections they come from. Do this exercise for all the

Hint: Before you start, separate your tiles into Suits, Dragons, Winds, and so on, so that it will be easier for you to select the specific tiles you need. When you finish putting a hand together, return the tiles back into Suits, and so on. Then, for the next hand, you can select the tiles you need without having to hunt randomly through all the tiles.

Sections of the card and you will have a firm start to learning the hands.

1. Describe to yourself what is necessary to complete the hand—how many different Suits, how many of each Suit, what numbers, and so on. Can you use Jokers? Check the Instructions to be sure you are doing the hand correctly.

2. Now select the tiles you need to complete the hand, placing them face up on your rack. Use Jokers if you like, where appropriate. When you have assembled all the necessary tiles, you have Mah Jongg. As you work through the hands, remember the Section the hand comes from and the individual hand.

> Please notice that *Mah Jongg requires* 14 tiles.

This exercise takes time and patience. I can assure you that if you practice it diligently, you will 1) find it easier to locate the Sections on the card, 2) find it easier to associate which kinds of tiles go with which Sections and 3) begin to remember certain hands.

Reminder: Jokers may be used only in a Pung, Kong, Quint or Sextet. You may *never* use or substitute a Joker for any two matching tiles (a Pair), or when a hand calls for a Single tile. For example, you may not use a Joker in the combination FF or in any combination that calls for a Pair of anything. The 2004 combination calls for a Pair of Soap Dragons (used as zeros) so you may not use a Joker. The 2 and 4 tiles are Single tiles so you can't use a Joker there either. Another example: NEWS isn't a kong, it's a combination of four Single tiles, so no Jokers are allowed.

✺ QUIZ ✺
Cracking the Code

1. What do the different colors on the card indicate?
2. Explain matching tiles.
3. Define opposite Dragon and matching Dragon.

4. In the Consecutive Run Section, what do 1s, 2s, 3s, 4s, and 5s indicate?

5. What does "Pung 8s Only" mean?

6. What do W and D mean?

7. Explain Like Numbers.

8. Explain what X and C refer to.

9. Can Jokers be used in the Singles and Pairs Section? In NEWS? Why?

10. If a hand repeats numbers or Dragons but in different colors, what does it mean?

11. What tiles are necessary for the 2nd hand in the 2004 Section? Read the Instructions next to the hand.

12. In the hand below, explain the Instruction "Pairs, Any Like Odd No."

    FF EEEE 11 11 WWWW

13. What tiles do you need for NEWS?

14. How many Suits are required for the 4th hand in the 13579 Section? What numbers?

15. What tiles are necessary to complete 4th hand in the 2468 Section?

16. Explain the Instruction "Kong 1, 3, or 5."

17. In the 369 Section, how many Suits and what numbers are needed for the 3rd hand?

18. In most Sections, the player must follow the numbers exactly as printed to complete the hand. In which Sections can the player choose the numbers to complete the hand?

19. What do the various Sections indicate about the tiles?

20. What do matching colors indicate?

21. If a hand is printed in Green and Red, do you have to use Bams and Craks, in that order?

22. How many tiles do you need for Mah Jongg?

23. Look at the 3rd hand in the Consecutive Run Section. These are the tiles I have chosen to complete the hand.

    44 55 777 888 9999

    Are they correct? Why?

24. Which Section and which hand is represented by the following tiles? (Hint: Which are odd numbers, even numbers, consecutive numbers, etc.?)

FF 5555 5555 5555

FFFF 6666 7777 DD

11 33 11 33 55 3333

555 7777 777 9999

33 44 333 444 5555

SSSSS DDDD 55555

FF 3333 6666 9999

2222 44 6666 88 88

222 DDDD 888 DDDD

NNNN E W SSSS 2004

25. In the Addition Hands Section, there is an "or" between the hands, a "+" sign and an "=" sign. Explain why.

ANSWERS

1. Different colors indicate different Suits and Dragons.

2. Matching tiles are tiles of the same Suit and number, same Dragon, same Wind, or same Flower. *Pair, Pung, Kong, Quint and Sextet are matching tiles.*

3. The term opposite Dragon refers to the Dragon that matches a third unused Suit. When the Suit and Dragon are the same color, the Dragon is said to be a matching Dragon.

4. The numbers indicate that ascending consecutive numbers are needed to complete the hands. You may use *any* ascending consecutive numbers.

5. It means you must use three matching 8s only.

6. W means West. D means Dragon.

7. Like Numbers are numbers that are all alike.

8. X indicates that a hand is Exposed and that you may call for a tile to expose a Pung, Kong, Quint or Sextet. C indicates a Concealed hand and you may not call for any tile, except the last tile you need for Mah Jongg.

9. No, because the tiles needed for that Section are all Singles and Pairs and you may not use Jokers for Single tiles or in any Pair. No, NEWS is four Single tiles.

(Answers continued on next page.)

ANSWERS *(cont.)*

10. It means you must use the same numbers or Dragons, but in different Suits.
11. The Instructions are clear. They call for 4 Green Dragons, 4 Red Dragons, and any matching Suit for 2 and 4.
12. The hand requires two Pairs of the same odd number (1, 3, 5, 7, *or* 9) in two different Suits.
13. North, East, West, South.
14. One. The Dragon is the same color as the Suit. Use the matching Dragon. 1s, 3s, and 5s.
15. A Pung of 2s in any one Suit and a Kong of its matching Dragon; next a Pung of 8s in any second Suit and a Kong of its matching Dragon.
16. It means you may choose one of the numbers indicated to Kong.
17. Like Pungs mean the numbers you Pung must be all alike—3s, 6s, *or* 9s. The hand requires 6 of the same number and Suit, but since there are only 4 of each number and suit, 2 Jokers are required.
18. The Consecutive Run (except the first two hands), Like Numbers, some hands in Quints, some hands in Singles and Pairs.
19. The Sections are groups of hands and each Section indicates what kinds and combinations of tiles are necessary to complete a hand.
20. Matching colors require matching Suits/Dragons. They also indicate which combinations belong together.
21. No. You choose the Suits and in what order to use them.

22. 14.
23. No. When the numbers in different colors are repeated, the same numbers in different Suits must be used. The hand calls for *three* ascending consecutive numbers. Ascending consecutive numbers would be 4s, 5s, 6s, not 4s, 5s, 7s, 8s, and 9s. The correct tiles should be **44 55 444 555 6666**.
24. • **Like Numbers** 1st hand
    • **Consecutive Run** 4th hand
    • **13579** 6th hand
    • **13579** 2nd hand
    • **Consecutive Run** 3rd hand
    • **Quints** 2nd hand
    • **369** 2nd hand
    • **2468** 5th hand
    • **2468** 4th hand
    • **2004** 3rd hand
25. "Or" means you may do either the hands in one Suit or in three Suits. The "+" and "=" signs are just indicating an addition equation. They are irrelevant. Notice that each of these hands needs a Pair of 1s to complete it.

⚬❦ CHAPTER 4 ❧⚬
Construction Project: The Wall

Now let's turn our attention to something a little less cerebral than learning the hands on the card. We are going to learn to build and then break what is called the **Wall**. This procedure provides the means to allow the player to pick the tiles needed for a hand. I always think of this part of the game as building the Great Wall of China. The Chinese call it the "Garden Wall," but to me the Great Wall seems a little more majestic.

Before we begin, let's look at the racks that come with a set, because they are an essential part of building the Wall. There are usually four racks, one for each player. There is a ridge on one side of the rack that will hold your tiles and a straight edge on the other side. At the end of the rack is a small projection that helps to keep the tiles in a proper line. The pegs at the end of the rack are used to hold betting chips, used in the Chinese version of the game. Place the rack in front of you with the ridge side facing you and the straight edge side facing the middle of the table.

A rack

❧ Build the Wall ❧

To build the Wall, all the tiles are turned face down and thoroughly mixed. This is, no doubt, why mah jongg is loosely translated to mean "clattering sparrows"—the mixing makes quite a racket. The Wall consists of four parts—each consisting of 38 tiles, placed in front of players' racks. Each player places two rows of 19 tiles, one row stacked on top of the other, along the straight edge side of the rack. That's 38 tiles in front of each player. Now we've built the Wall.

Note: Racks are notoriously made too short to hold a row of 19 tiles, so some of the tiles will overhang.

38 tiles: 2 rows of 19 tiles

In Chinese mah jongg, the direction you sit at the table, North, South, East or West, is important, because of the rules of scoring if you win. In Chinese mah jongg, East is the advantageous position. But in American mah jongg, there is no advantage, or disadvantage, to sitting East. Anyone can be "East," and usually the host or hostess is the person designated as East. It is important in American mah jongg, because in the beginning, East breaks the Wall, ends up picking 14 tiles from the Wall (everyone else ends up picking 13), and starts the play of the game.

❧ Break the Wall ❧

Now let's examine why and how the Wall gets broken.

The Wall is broken by separating it into two parts; one part is used for players to pick the tiles for their potential hands. The other part serves as the last section of the Wall in the game from which players pick new tiles. The point of separation is arbitrarily determined by a roll of the dice.

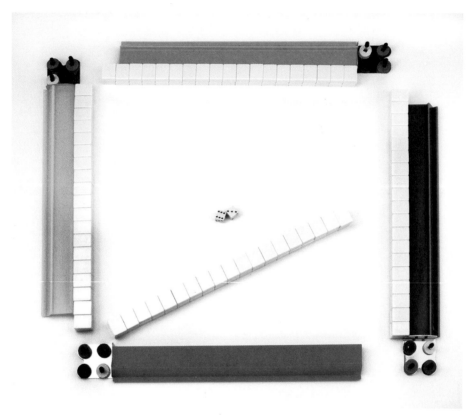

East's Wall in the center of the table

Here's how this procedure works. The player who is East rolls the pair of dice (included with all sets) and makes a mental note of the number rolled. (Be sure to place the dice into the rack of the player to the right because this player will be East for the next game.) Let's say East rolls a nine, then places the dice into the next East's rack.

With the aid of the rack, East's Wall of 38 tiles is pushed to the center of the table, on a diagonal, with the right side of the Wall out in front. East then counts the number of tiles in the Wall that corresponds to the number rolled

East returns 9 tiles to the rack.

on the dice. In our example, East rolled a nine. So the count of nine begins, from the right side of the Wall. East counts "1, 2, 3, 4, 5, 6, 7, 8, 9" two-tiered stacks, separates these 18 (9 x 2 = 18) tiles from the rest of the Wall (the "break" point), and slides them back to the straight edge side of the rack. Just leave them placed against the rack. This is the last section of the Wall that will be used later in the game.

Now we have nine two-tiered tiles separated from the Wall and replaced on the straight edge side of East's rack. The rest of the East's Wall remains in the center of the table.

East now picks two two-tiered stacks (four tiles) from the Wall, starting from the right or "broken" edge, and places them face down on the ridged side of his or her rack. The player to the right of East picks the next two stacks (four tiles) and places them face down. The third player picks the next four tiles, and so on, for three rounds until everyone has 12 tiles. These tiles should be placed face down, in front of you. They are the tiles that will start your hand.

There usually are not enough tiles in East's Wall for all the players to pick 12 tiles. So when all the tiles from East's broken Wall have been picked, in order

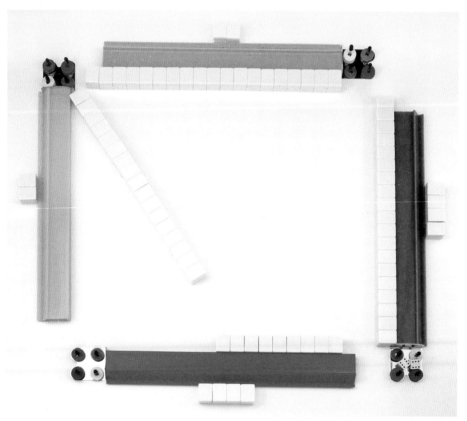

A new Wall comes from the left of East.

to make sure everyone gets the proper number of tiles, the next 38 tiles of the Wall must be pushed to the center of the table. These 38 tiles come from the Wall of the player to the *left* of East.

Now, the player to the left of East uses his or her rack to push the Wall to

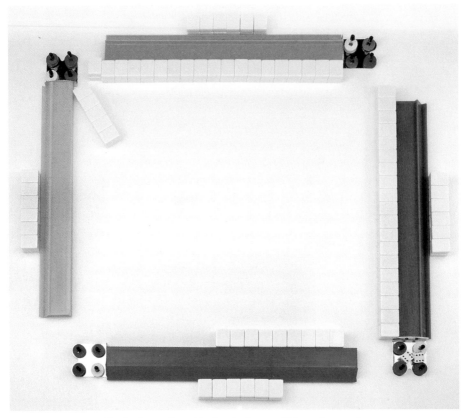

Each player has 12 tiles in front of his or her rack.

the center of the table, again with the right side of the Wall diagonally in front. The picking of tiles continues, again from right to left, counterclockwise around the table.

Everyone now has 12 tiles.

How does East get 14 tiles? East now picks the first and third tiles from the top tier of the Wall *only,* making a total of 14 tiles.

Everyone else must now pick one more tile to make a total of 13 tiles in his or her hand. Since East picked two tiles from the top tier of the Wall, there will be one odd tile left at the broken edge and one more odd tile

One word of etiquette: Wait until everyone has the proper number of tiles before placing your tiles on your rack.

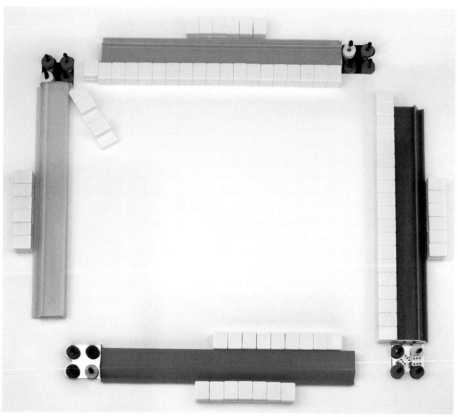

East has picked the first and third tiles from the top tier.

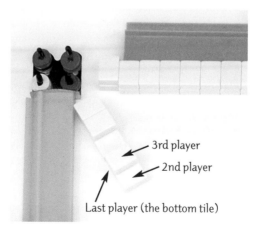

3rd player
2nd player
Last player (the bottom tile)

Picking the 13th tile: The second player picks the outermost bottom tile; the third player picks the next top tile; the last player picks the next bottom tile.

left further in the Wall itself. So the next player picks the first outermost odd tile, the next player picks the next top tile, and the next player picks the outermost bottom tile, leaving the last odd tile. Now everyone has 13 tiles. (People always ask, "Why is it done this way?" and I answer, "It's just one of the mysteries of mah jongg.") Everyone now places his or her tiles face up onto the ridged side of the racks.

 DO IT   Build and break the Wall and pick your tiles several times so that you can be comfortable with doing this. The repetition of picking tiles in the proper sequence will teach you that *picking tiles always comes from the right of East (counterclockwise) and that new Walls always come from the left of East (clockwise).*

Everyone now has 13 tiles face up on his or her rack, while East has 14. What do you do now? We are going to learn what to do with the conglomeration of tiles in front of you—the nitty-gritty of "How to Select Your Hand," the next stop on our journey.

⚗ QUIZ ⚗

Construction Project: The Wall

1. How many tiles does each player place in front of the rack when building the Wall?
2. After East rolls the dice, from which side of the Wall does the count start, right or left?
3. After East picks the first four tiles, which player picks the next tiles?
4. How many tiles at a time does each player pick? How many tiles does each player end up with for a hand?
5. How does East select the last tiles needed to make 14?
6. Which player's Wall gets pushed to the center of the table when East's Wall is gone?

7. From which direction do players pick tiles?

8. From which direction do new Walls come?

ANSWERS

1. Two stacks of 19 tiles, or a total of 38 tiles.
2. The count starts from the right side.
3. The player to East's right.
4. Four tiles. 13, while East picks 14.
5. East picks the first and third tiles from the top tier of the Wall.
6. The player to the left of East pushes his or her Wall to the center of the table.
7. Players pick tiles from the right of East.
8. New Walls come from the left of East.

❧ CHAPTER 5 ☙

What Do I Do Now?
How to Select Your Hand

Beginning players report that the most difficult and daunting part of the game is finding a hand from the fifty or so possible choices on the card. I confess, at first, making order out of the chaos of tiles just picked from the Wall isn't easy. I often hear the lament "I don't have anything." Or if by some chance a beginner does find a possible hand, a common complaint is "But I don't have four Flowers!" No, you don't. In fact, you don't have *lots* of tiles you need for a Mah Jongg hand. The tiles you've just picked from the Wall are the bits and pieces of a potential *start*, a *nucleus* of a hand—not the end. In this part of the game, you are only beginning to put a possible hand together.

Furthermore, the Charleston (which we'll learn about in the next chapter) is a companion to this chapter, and will allow you to acquire new tiles to help in determining your hand. So keep that in mind, because at this point, your choices are tentative—not written in stone.

But, you might wonder, how do experienced players put their tiles together for a hand in a blink of the eye? There's no magic wand or abracadabra. These "Mah Jongg mavens" know the hands on the Card; they organize their tiles (we'll see how); and they pay attention to important "Power" tiles (see below).

Let's go step by step through how to find a hand, simply and easily, from the seemingly disparate mess in front of you. We'll first discuss the general ideas you need to understand. Then we'll do several practice examples.

Note: The information in this chapter is relevant to any NMJL card you might use, but the specific hands we'll refer to are found on the 2004 card (from the back of the book) that we used in Chapter 3.

❧ Organize Your Tiles ❧

The great mistake that many beginners make after they pick Wall tiles, is to immediately look for a hand. This is a mistake because before you look for a hand you must first find the Section or category your tiles match; *the Section(s) will lead you to your hand(s)*. Finding a hand within a Section is a plus. At this stage of the game, all you need is a Section.

Look at the card and notice that in all Sections the hands are organized by numbers *and* Suits—not just by numbers alone. And the numbers of the hands go *up*...1, 2, 3, 4, 5... 3, 6, 9... 2, 4, 6, 8. Even in the Addition hands, the (first) numbers go up: 2+9, 3+8, 4+7.

So first, organize your tiles on the rack the same way the card's hands are organized: (1) By numbers *and* suits, and (2) Going *up*. This gives you an idea of how many Suits there are in the hand, if there is a lot of one Suit, lots of Flowers, matching/opposite Dragons, Winds or Jokers. In addition, and most importantly, it reveals the "Power tiles," combinations—Pairs, Pungs, etc.— that are the strength of your hand and are crucial to selecting your specific Section and hand. We'll discuss this idea a little later on.

Next, find a Section. The Sections that your tiles represent will become obvious when you separate and place all the odd numbers together on your rack (13579 Section), separate and place all your even numbers together on your rack (2468 Section), and arrange them for the 369 Section, the Consecutive Run Section, and so on.

Then, count the number of tiles you have in each Section. A viable Section should contain at least five tiles. Six or seven is a stronger start. But sometimes you end up with Sections with only three or four tiles each. That's not such a strong start, but it's better than nothing, and remember—it's not the end. When you count, be sure to include Jokers and/or Flowers. They are an essential part of hands!

But keep your mind open. *If you don't find enough tiles for a viable Section, reorganize your tiles to reflect another Section.* Remember, there are at least nine Sections on the card. Start with the most common ones (which we discuss below) but don't forget the other five or six. And let me emphasize again: *All you need at this stage is a Section or Sections.*

Note that the most commonly followed Sections for a hand are the odd numbers (1, 3, 5, 7, 9), the even numbers (2, 4, 6, 8), the Consecutive Run numbers (1, 2, 3, 4, 5, 4, 5, 6, 7... 2, 3, 2, 3, 4), and the 369 numbers. So these are the ones we'll start with.

We'll use three examples of 13 tiles, randomly picked from the Wall, to illustrate the ideas we've just discussed.

Example 1: **1, 4 Crak 3, 5, 5, 8 Dot 2, 6, 7, 9 Bam N E W**

 DO IT   *1. Set up tiles on your rack to match Example 1.*

 DO IT   2. *Now, organize the tiles* by separating odd numbers, even numbers, 369 numbers, etc. by Suits and numbers that go *up*, just like the hands on the card do.
(Odd) **1 Crak 3, 5, 5 Dot** **7, 9 Bam**
(Even) **2, 6 Bam** **4 Crak** **8 Dot**
(369) **3 Dot** **6, 9 Bam**
(Consecutive Run) **1, 4 Crak** **2 Bam** **3, 5, 5 Dot**
(Winds/Dragons) **N E W**

3. Count the tiles in each Section. The Odd and Consecutive Run Sections both have six tiles.

Example 2: **1, 9 Dot** 3, 4, 4 Bam **1, 2, 5, 5, 6 Crak S S   D (Soap)**

 1. Set up tiles on your rack to match Example 2.

 2. Separate the tiles into Sections.
(Odd) **1, 9 Dot** 3 Bam **1, 5, 5 Crak**
(Even) **2, 6 Crak** 4, 4 Bam
(Consecutive Run) **1 Dot** 3, 4, 4 Bam **1, 2, 5, 5, 6 Crak**
(Winds/Dragons) **D S, S**

 3. Count the tiles in each Section. The Consecutive Run Section has nine tiles.

Example 3: **1, 3, 6, 7 Dot** 2, 9 Bam **2, 9, 9 Crak J   F   N   E**

 1. Set up tiles on your rack to match Example 3.

 2. Separate the tiles into Sections.
(Odd) **1, 3, 7 Dot** 9, 9 Crak **9 Bam J   F**
(Even) **2 Crak** 2 Bam **6 Dot J   F**
(369) **3, 6 Dot** 9, 9 Crak **9 Bam J   F**

3. *Count the tiles in each Section.* Example 3 is a toss-up between the 369 Section (seven tiles) and the Odd Section (eight tiles).

❧ Power Tiles ❧

After a Section is determined, the next thing you must look for are "Power" tiles. What are they?

Power tiles are **Pairs, Pungs, Kongs of any tiles, including Flowers and/or Jokers**. They are the core component around which to build your hand. But you need to find other tiles that are "closely related" to them. And the hand in the Section you choose must mirror a hand on the Card. If there is no hand to match your tiles, you cannot win.

"Closely related" tiles are those connected by Suit *and* number/Dragon that reflect a hand on the Card. Although tiles may be related by numbers, and/or by Suits, if there's no hand that requires them, they are not an asset and not "closely related."

As an example, let's say your tiles include, among others, 2 Bam, 4 Bam, 9 Bam, and 2 Dot. The 2 Bam is "closely related" to the 4 Bam, but not to the 9 Bam, even though they all belong to the Bam Suit. There are Sections and hands that use 2 Bam and 4 Bam together, but none that use a 2 Bam or a 4 Bam with a 9 Bam. And 2 Bam and 2 Dot are related by number but not by Suit. They're not "closely related," unless there's a hand that uses 2 Bams and 2 Dots. Then they become "closer," so to speak. But if the hand you choose uses 2 Bam but not the 2 Dots, they are unrelated and of no value to your hand.

Once more, remember, this is just the beginning of the search for a hand. Be aware that you will have many missing tiles. And don't forget: your tiles must match a hand on the Card.

Let's go back to our first example, to recognize and learn how to benefit from Power tiles.

Example 1: **1, 4 Crak 3, 5, 5, 8 Dot** 2, 6, 7, 9 Bam **N E W**
(Odd) **1 Crak 3, 5, 5 Dot** 7, 9 Bam
(Consecutive Run) **1, 4, Crak** 2 Bam **3, 5, 5 Dot**
(Even) 2, 6 Bam **4 Crak 8 Dot**
(369) **3 Dot** 6, 9 Bam
(Winds/Dragons) **N E W**

In Example 1, both the Odd and the Consecutive Run Sections have six tiles, including *a Pair of 5 Dots*. This Pair is the "Power" around which to build the hand.

These two Sections both use 5s. In the Odd Section, there are a couple of hands that use the 1 Crak and the 3, 5, 5, Dot together (the 2nd) and the "OR" hand that uses the Pair of 5 Dot and the 7, 9 Bam (the 2nd). It's only four "closely related" tiles—not five or six, yet. Although these tiles do not offer strong beginning hands, they offer a *decisive Section* that may lead to a strong hand. At this point in the game, *all you need is a Section*. Having a hand in mind is a plus, but it's not the essential thing.

There are no "closely related" tiles in the Consecutive Run Section, because there is no hand that matches these tiles. Since all I need to begin with is a Section, even though there is no very strong hand yet, *I will concentrate on the Odd numbered 13579 Section, because there are potential hands that use the Power Pair.*

1 Crak 3, 5, 5 Dot (2nd hand)

5, 5 Dot 7, 9 Bam (the "OR" 2nd hand)

Let's look at Example 2. There are nine Consecutive Run tiles: a strong Section.

Example 2: **1, 9 Dot** 3, 4, 4 Bam **1, 2, 5, 5, 6 Crak S S D (Soap)**
(Consecutive Run) **1 Dot** 3, 4, 4 Bam **1, 2, 5, 5, 6 Crak**
(Odd) **1, 9 Dot** 3 Bam **1, 5, 5 Crak**
(Even) **2, 6 Crak** 4, 4 Bam
(Winds/Dragons) **D S, S**

The outstanding feature of this hand is the two Power Pairs—a Pair of 4 Bams and a Pair of 5 Craks—closely related by number but not by Suit.

Further inspection reveals a 3 Bam that is "closely related" to the 4 Bams, and a 6 Crak that is "closely related" to the 5 Craks because in the Consecutive

> *Tip:* Odd numbers and even numbers most often match a hand in the Consecutive Run Section.

Run Section, the 2nd hand requires *any* four consecutive numbers in any two Suits. Utilizing the "Power" tiles—the two Pairs—that hand matches my tiles. Counting six tiles toward a Mah Jongg hand is a very respectable beginning:

3, 4, 4 Bam 5, 5, 6 Crak

Additionally, the 1, 2 Crak 3, 4, 4 Bam can be used for the same hand but with different numbers. But in this hand only one Power Pair is utilized and uses only five tiles.

The 1st Consecutive hand uses four tiles and again, only one Pair, and is weak:

1, 2, 5, 5

What about the 13579 Section? The closest "relative" to the Pair of 5 Craks is 1 Crak. 3 Bam is related to the Power Pair (in the 2nd hand) but three tiles toward a hand is too weak to consider as a potential. The Odd Section is weak, even though there is a Pair of 5 Craks. The Pair of Souths has only one "relative," a D: again, a non-starter. The Even Section hands are also weak.

So, I am going to focus my primary attention on the 2nd hand in the Consecutive Run Section that uses both Power Pairs...and my secondary attention on the other hand that uses only one Power Pair.

3, 4, 4 Bam 5, 5, 6 Crak (2nd hand)

1, 2 Crak 3, 4, 4 Bam (2nd hand)

Now for Example 3. Let's consider the Odd Section (eight tiles), the 369 Section (seven tiles)...and now maybe the Consecutive Run Section, which has only five tiles, but also uses the Power Pair.

Example 3:   **1, 3, 6, 7 Dot   2, 9 Bam   2, 9, 9 Crak   J   F   N   E**

(Odd)   **F   1, 3, 7 Dot   J   9, 9 Crak   9 Bam**

(369)   **F   3, 6 Dot   J   9, 9 Crak   9 Bam**

(Consecutive Run)   **6, 7 Dot   J   9, 9 Crak**

There are eight tiles in the Odd Section. The Power Pair is 9 Crak. And the hand contains a valuable Joker.

Look for hands that use 9s. Are there any tiles "closely related" to the Pair? Any 5s or 7s Crak? No. But when the Joker is converted to a 5 Bam, voilà, I have "created" a hand (the 3rd) that uses the Power Pair that is five tiles strong:

1, 3 Dot   J (5 Bam)   99 Crak   (3rd hand)

Is there a hand that uses 7 Dot and the Pair of 9 Crak? If the Joker is now converted to a 5 Dot, yes, the "OR" 2nd hand also uses the Power Pair. But it is only four tiles. Neither hand requires Flowers.

J (5 Dot), 7 Dot   99 Crak   (2nd hand)

The Odd Section has yielded two hands, both using the Power Pair. Lean toward the stronger five-tile hand.

In the 369 Section, the first thing that stands out is the 3, 6 Dot, and again, the Power Pair of 9 Craks and a 9 Bam. Plus a versatile Joker and a Flower. That's six tiles, maybe seven. Look for possible hands in the 369 Section that use Flowers. There are three. But the last hand in the 369 Section comes the closest, because *I convert the Joker into a 9 Dot, and utilize the Flower and the Power Pair*, making six tiles toward a Maj Jongg hand. Very respectable, and so far, the strongest Section/hand.

F   3, 6, J (9 Dot)   99 Crak   (6th hand)

In the Consecutive Run Section, a close search reveals that the Consecutive Run hand (the 2nd) is definitely a hand to be considered because again, converting the Joker to an 8 Crak allows me to use the Power Pair and gives me five tiles toward Mah Jongg.

6, 7 Dot J (8 Crak) 9, 9 Crak (2nd hand)

This example shows the power that Jokers have to help you create hands from seemingly unrelated elements. They also strengthen a chosen Section/hand(s). That's why Jokers are a valuable asset and must be included as an integral part of your selection.

All the hands in three different Sections have utilized the Power Pair in this example. Remember that we said that the Charleston (coming up next!) might help determine the choice of the Section/hand? So, this hand says "Keep your options open."

But what to do when you have no Power tiles, as is sometimes the case? When nothing seems to go with anything? Go ahead and organize your tiles by Section—Odds, Evens, etc.—by Suit and numbers that go *up*. Go to the Section with the greatest number and look for closely related tiles. And don't forget to use Jokers to create hands. Do the same with hands that have a predominance of one Suit, seven, eight or more. At this point, all you need is a Section.

HINTS: If you have lots of Jokers, three or four (it happens), look in the Quint Section, because you must have several Jokers for those hands.

When you have disparate combinations that don't fit with your other tiles, keep them until the Charleston is completed or until you have made a firm decision that they are not useful.

Several different Dragons should trigger you to search the Winds-Dragons Section. The same is true for Winds. But one North and one East do not a beginning make!

A run of, say, 4 5 6, 6 7 8, 1 2 3 consecutive numbers is not a hand on the card when there are no other tiles to go with it.

❧ EXERCISE ☙
Select Your Hand

This next exercise is essential and reinforces all the ideas we've just discussed. Do this exercise many, many times—until you can look at your tiles and easily go to the Sections and hands that might be appropriate.

 Turn all the tiles face down, mix them, and pick 13 tiles at random. Place them on your rack. Then:

1. Organize the tiles by Suit *and* number (going *up* the scale), Dragon, Wind, Flower and Joker.

2. Reorganize the tiles by Section: Odds, Evens, 369, Consecutive Run, and so on. Mirror the way the Card's hands are arranged: by Suits and numbers, going *up*.

3. Focus on the Section(s) using the greatest number of your tiles—at least five or six.

4. Focus on hand(s) in that Section(s) that most closely match (ideally) at least five or six of your tiles.

   a. Build your hand(s) around the Power tiles and other "close relatives."

   b. Use Jokers to create and strengthen hands.

5. Remember, this is just the beginning! You'll still be left with a lot of missing tiles. Be flexible, and keep your options (and mind) open.

And now, I invite you to the Charleston—and I don't mean the dance!

❧ CHAPTER 6 ☙

Cha, Cha, Charleston

In American mah jongg, the Charleston is the name given to the process of passing unwanted tiles to the other players. Why the Charleston? I like to think it's a reference to the dance that swept the country in the 1920s just like mah jongg did.

Passing your unwanted tiles to the other players and getting their unwanted tiles offers the opportunity to improve or change your hand. Hopefully, the Charleston can increase the possibility of winning by enhancing your hand or leading you to another, better hand. So keep this purpose in mind as you go through the process of passing and keeping tiles. You might think of the Charleston as a "passing fancy" or "fancy passing." (*Ouch!*)

First, let's review. The player has picked 13 tiles (or 14 for East), separated them according to the guidelines in the previous chapter, and has come to a tentative decision about the Sections or hands he or she might want to play. Do not despair if the hand looks pretty bleak. Things are about to change.

All players do the Charleston simultaneously. It consists of three separate passes, with each pass requiring three tiles. The first pass goes to the player on your right, the next pass to the player opposite you, and finally the last pass to the player on your left. These three passes are compulsory. It's called the First Charleston, because there is potential for another round of passing—an optional Second Charleston.

Most often, a Second Charleston proceeds, this time going in the opposite direction of the First Charleston. Again, three separate passes are required with three tiles to each pass. You begin with the player on your left, then to the player opposite, and finally to the player on your right. If you complete both the First and Second Charleston, that's six passes in all.

The Charleston is followed by an optional Courtesy pass, making a possible total of seven passes. Each pass, except the Courtesy, must contain any three tiles, except a Joker. Jokers may not be passed in the Charleston or exchanged in the Courtesy.

⁂ The First Charleston ⁂

First, select three tiles, that are unwanted and unrelated to your hand. Place them face down, and pass them to the player on your *right*. Now you take the three tiles passed to you, look at them, and decide if any of them help your hand. Keep the ones that do. They now become part of your hand.

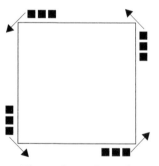

Three tiles to the right

Next, take three more unwanted tiles and pass them, face down, to the player *opposite* you.

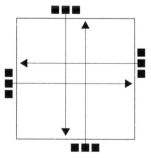

Three tiles opposite

DO IT

Look at the tiles passed to you and decide if any of them add to your hand. Again, keep the ones you want. Once more, pass three unwanted tiles face down to the player on your *left* (called **First Left**) and keep the tiles passed to you. Or you can **steal** or **blind pass**.

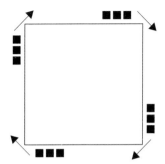

Three tiles to the left (First Left)

✌ Steal or Blind Pass ✌

You must always pass three tiles in the Charleston. But sometimes, after two passes, your hand offers two very good potential hands and you don't have or you can't find three tiles to pass. There is an alternative. You may choose to **steal** or **blind pass** one, two, or three tiles.

Let's say you can only find two tiles in your hand to pass. *Without looking at it*, take one of the tiles just passed to you and add it to the two unwanted tiles you have to pass. Now you have the three tiles you need to pass; pass them. If you only want to pass one tile, take two tiles from the ones passed to you and add them to make the three tiles you need, and pass them. You keep the other tiles, being sure you still have 13 (or 14) tiles. Again, you must not look at the tiles you take to make up your three-tile total. That's why it's called stealing or a blind pass.

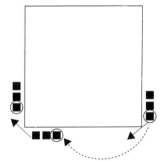

Steal: One stolen tile (from the player to your right) is added to two unwanted tiles from your hand, to make the three tiles required to pass to the player on your left.

This is the completion of the First Charleston, which is compulsory—a pass to the right, a pass opposite, and a pass to the left.

At this point, *any* player may stop the First Charleston from continuing to the second by announcing a wish to stop. Say, "I want to stop." You don't need to justify or explain your action. The passing stops, no ifs, ands, or buts. A Courtesy follows (see below).

Stopping the Charleston can happen and occasionally does.

Why would a player want to stop the Charleston and give up the opportunity to perhaps acquire more needed tiles? Because after the First Charleston, his or her hand may be such that the player can't find three tiles to pass, or doesn't want to pass three tiles. The hand may have six tiles for one hand and six tiles for another and the player doesn't want to make a decision that might weaken one hand over the other. Or, he or she already has 10 or 11 tiles toward Mah Jongg. In these situations, stealing is not an option. Because before being able to steal again, the player needs to complete two more passes of three tiles each from his or her hand in the Second Charleston. So the player stops after the First Charleston.

Usually, however, no one wants to stop, so a **Second Charleston** proceeds, *in the reverse direction from the first.*

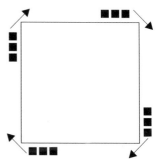

Again, select three unwanted tiles from your hand, pass them face down, to the player on your *left* (called the **Second Left**), and look at the tiles passed to you.

Three tiles to the left (Second Left)

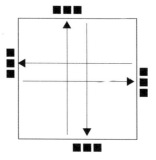

Pass three more unwanted tiles to the player *opposite*; look again at the tiles passed to you.

Three tiles opposite

Finally, pass three more unwanted tiles to the player on your *right* (called the **Last Right**) and keep the tiles passed to you.

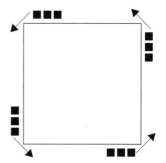

Three tiles to the right (Last Right)

On the last right, again you may choose to steal or blind pass.

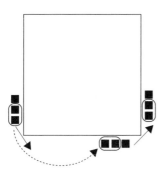

Steal: Two stolen tiles from the player to your left are added to one unwanted tile from your hand, to make the three tiles that you are required to pass to the player on your right.

This is the completion of the Second Charleston.

Hint: To make it easier to remember the sequences of the Charleston, sometimes the acronym **ROLLOR** is used. It stands for **R**ight, **O**pposite, **L**eft–**L**eft, **O**pposite, **R**ight.

⟡ Courtesy ⟡

You still have one more opportunity to acquire new tiles. It's called **Courtesy**. A Courtesy always follows a Charleston. If the passing stops after the First Charleston, a Courtesy follows. If it doesn't, a Courtesy follows at the completion of the Second Charleston—only one Courtesy is allowed. At the end of either the First Charleston or the Second Charleston, by mutual agreement with the player opposite, you may exchange zero, one, two, or three tiles. Ask, "Would you like to do a Courtesy?" and "How many tiles would you like?" The player with whom you do the Courtesy may want a fewer number of tiles than you do. In that case, you always agree to the lesser amount. For example, if you want to exchange three tiles and the other player only wants to exchange one...you exchange one.

That's the "dance." After a couple of hints and a brief summary, we'll discuss some strategies for the Charleston.

⊷ Hints ⊷

1. Never pass a Pair of anything. Break it up into two passes. Pairs are not easy to acquire. Don't help your opponents!

2. Do not pass Flowers, unless you have no other choice. Lots of hands require Flowers. Again, don't help your opponents.

3. You may not look at the tiles passed to you until you've passed your three tiles.

4. Remember, you can only steal on the *first left pass in the First Charleston* and on the *last right pass in the Second Charleston*.

Summary of the Charleston

⊛ You must always pass three tiles at a time in the Charleston.

⊛ Do not look at the tiles passed to you before you pass your tiles.

⊛ **First Charleston**:
   • Right, Opposite, Left—you may steal (sometimes called **First Left**).
   • First Charleston is compulsory.

⬢ **Second Charleston** (Reverse of the First):
  - Left, **O**pposite, **R**ight—you may steal (sometimes called **Last Right**).
  - Second Charleston is optional.

⬢ One **Courtesy** Only
  - Exchange zero, one, two, or three tiles with the opposite player.
  - Follows either the First or Second Charleston.

⬢ **Blind Pass** or **Steal**
  - This is allowed twice—on the **First Left** pass and/or the **Last Right** pass.
  - Add one, two, or three tiles from the tiles passed to you, without looking at them, to make the three tiles required to pass to the next player.

❧ What to Pass ☙

Pass tiles that are not connected to the potential hand you've chosen—tiles you don't need or want. Do not pass a Pair of anything. Instead break it up into two different passes. Try desperately not to pass Flowers.

Sometimes after you arrange your tiles, you may find they don't hold much promise and you can't find a viable Section or hand. Don't spend a lot of time and energy trying to decide what to pass. Simply find any three tiles that do not go with any other tiles and pass them. Remember, you have seven chances to get tiles that can be a start of a hand.

3 unrelated tiles to pass

Pass tiles that don't improve or significantly change your hand, even if you are tempted to keep them. Don't clutter your hand (or mind) with tiles that have little relation to other tiles in your hand. Collecting two or three tiles that might be used for a different hand, but are unrelated to your other tiles, is not a good strategy. Ask yourself, "Does this tile strengthen my hand?" If the answer is "No," then pass it.

As you acquire new tiles, check the card to make sure there is a hand that corresponds to your tiles. If you have collected tiles for a hand that doesn't exist, you cannot hope to win. Don't keep tiles just because they look wonderful together or you just like them. If there is no hand on the card to go with some of your tiles, get rid of them and look elsewhere. Even if you do not have a specific hand in mind, you should still be able to pick out the one or two hands that most closely match your tiles.

Many times, though, you will get tiles that are related and could indeed be used for another hand. Should you keep them or not? The first thing to do is *count* to see which hand uses the greater number of tiles. When you count, include any Jokers, Flowers, and Dragons you have that the hands may require. If there are more tiles for one hand than the other, go for that hand.

But what if you have the same number of tiles that are potentially useful in both hands? You have to pass three tiles, but you can only find one or two. And you can't steal. You are faced with a common dilemma.

You can't keep everything! You will have to make a decision. But you need to take into account such things as: Which hand do I feel more comfortable with? Does one hand require Pairs I don't already have? Do I have the Pairs I need? Can I use Jokers? Where? Is one hand easier to make? The kinds of tiles going around in the Charleston (Odds? Evens? Winds?) can have a bearing on your choice of a hand. For example, if you are looking at a hand in the 13579 Section and the tiles you're getting in the Charleston are mostly even numbers, you might conclude that others are also playing odd numbered hands. You might want to consider switching your hand to another Section and keep the even numbered tiles if you can. Finally, you may decide just to take a chance on one hand over the other.

There are many factors you will have to weigh. When you first begin to do the Charleston, don't agonize over lost opportunities. Your mistakes will teach you for the next time. But you still have to think! If you have to pass a tile you think you will need, keep your fingers crossed and hope it comes back. Sometimes it does. It's also a good idea to keep your options open. If one hand doesn't work out, you'll still have other choices.

Some beginners express concern that they are passing tiles another player may need. This is a legitimate concern. For example, if you passed Wind tiles and they don't come back around, you might logically assume someone is saving Winds. Naturally, you don't want to pass more Wind tiles. You absolutely don't want to pass Flower tiles (unless you're desperate) and *never* pass Pairs of tiles. But as a beginner, you need to primarily focus on your own hand and collecting the tiles that you need. At this stage, you don't want to jeopardize your hand because you think another player may need some tile you have to pass. Until you gain a little experience playing the game, you'll do best to concentrate on your own hand.

❧ What to Keep ❧

Keep the tiles that strengthen your choice or choices of potential hands, and that are related to your Section and hand. Once you have an idea about what Section and hand you will be playing, you have an idea about what tiles to keep and what tiles to pass.

Many beginners mistakenly keep tiles that do not go with the hands they have chosen. Look at these examples to help you avoid this common error.

You have decided to focus in on the 2468 Section. You are looking for even numbers. Someone passes an odd numbered tile. You keep it because the Suit matches other tiles in your hand. But an odd numbered tile does not help an even numbered hand! You should not keep it. When you are playing the 369 Section, keep 3s, 6s, and 9s. You are not interested in 7s, 8s, 4s, or 2s, even though the Suits may match. Pass them. Don't keep even numbered tiles if you are playing a 13579 hand. If your hand calls for Green Dragons, don't keep Red

Hint: After you have arranged your tiles to reflect a Section, the numbers on your tiles can help you decide what to keep. For example, let's say you have eight odd-numbered tiles and when you rearrange them (up the scale and in numbers and Suits that go together) you notice that you have mostly 5s, 7s, and 9s. Then don't keep the 1s, or 3s. Look for hands that require 5s, 7s, and 9s and tiles that help that hand.

Dragons and Soap Dragons, as they do not help your hand. *Don't be tempted to keep tiles unrelated to your hand.*

If you decide on a hand, stick with it!

As you gain experience and knowledge of the hands, it will be easier for you to keep alternative hands in mind, but as a beginner, it can be confusing. Once you are fairly sure you have found a hand you want to play, focus on what tiles strengthen it. Keep those and pass the others. Stay with the hand you've chosen!

❧ At the End of the Charleston, Reassess ❧

At the end of the Charleston reassess your hand, because frequently new tiles will lead you from your originally selected Section and/or hand to another. Conversely, the tiles you've received in the Charleston will have strengthened your original hand. In either case, in an overwhelming majority of times, you will have a hand in mind by the end of the Charleston. Many times, the Charleston provides!

Sometimes, you may find that you have ended up with two potential hands. In that case as you play, new tiles will lead you to choose one hand over the other. The importance of being familiar with the hands on the card becomes apparent, because the more familiar you are with them, the easier it will be to make a choice.

Before you start to play, think about how many and what tiles you are missing—where you might use Jokers, do you need Pairs, and what options remain open. Many times, as the game progresses, you will find that the hand you started out to play may not be the hand you end up playing. I know it's a lot for a beginner to keep in mind, but it's something you will eventually need to do. As you gain experience, these things will become almost automatic, but give it a try now, anyway.

Selecting your hand and the Charleston go together and you need to practice them together. Try this exercise, using the procedures you've learned in these two chapters.

✁ EXERCISE ✁
Select Your Hand, & The Charleston

Turn the tiles face down and mix them up. Select 13 (or 14) tiles randomly and place them on your rack. **Do the four steps** outlined in Chapter 5 for selecting your hand, and after you've made a tentative decision, **do the Charleston** by picking three tiles from your hand and randomly exchanging them with three other tiles on the table. Do this six times and then **do a Courtesy** of one, two, or three tiles. As you select new tiles, remember to keep asking yourself, "Does this tile help my hand?" If yes, keep it. If no, pass it. If you happen to pick a Joker, put it back and select another tile. (Jokers can't be passed in the Charleston, remember?) Most of the time you will end up with one or two potential hands.

As you practice selecting your hand and the Charleston together, you will begin to be more comfortable and confident about your choices. And after you complete the Charleston, if you still haven't reached a firm decision about your hand, you will have lots of opportunities to shape a hand as you play the game.

✁ ✁

We've come a long way from identifying the tiles, becoming familiar with the card, building and breaking the Wall, tentatively deciding on a hand, and finally completing the Charleston. Congratulations!

And now, the last stop on our journey is in sight. The next chapter will deal with the actual playing of the game, putting all of the skills we've learned in the previous chapters to good use. It's on to "The Play's the Thing"!

You might want to do the quiz to make sure you understand this material.

✺ QUIZ ✺

Cha, Cha, Charleston

1. How many tiles at a time must you pass in the Charleston?
2. The First Charleston goes to the player on your right, the player opposite you, and then the player on your left. Describe the Second Charleston.
3. What is Courtesy? When do you do it? What is the maximum number of tiles you may exchange? The minimum?
4. Explain a blind pass or stealing. When can you use it?
5. True or False? Only East can stop the Charleston.
6. Is it mandatory to complete two Charlestons?
7. In the Charleston, can you pass a Pair? Flowers? Jokers?

ANSWERS

1. Three.
2. The Second Charleston is the reverse of the first—the player to your left, the player opposite you, and the player to your right.
3. After completing the Charleston, the opposite players may request a further exchange of zero, one, two, or three tiles. Courtesy follows a Charleston, after either the First or Second Charleston is completed. The maximum number of tiles a player can exchange is three and the minimum is zero.
4. A player needs three tiles to pass. If three tiles are unavailable, it is permissible to take the necessary number of tiles just passed to the player to make three. These tiles may not be looked at. You may steal on the First Left pass and on the Last Right pass of the Charleston.
5. False.
6. No.
7. Yes, but not advisable. Yes, but not advisable—do it only when you have no other choice. No.

ꙮ CHAPTER 7 ꙮ

The Play's the Thing

The play's the thing we've been aiming for. So here we go, at long last! But first, let's briefly go over the stops on our journey that have brought us here. You have picked 13 (or 14) tiles, arranged your tiles, gone through the Charleston and Courtesy, reassessed the possibilities, and arrived at a decision on a hand. *Whew!* Now, let's get to it!

ꙮ The Game ꙮ

A brief summary of the game will give you an idea of how it's played. Once again, the object of the game is to be the first to complete the combinations of tiles that match the hand you've chosen from the card. Players pick and discard tiles to complete these combinations, and the first player to do so, wins. It sounds simple, but in mah jongg, there are many restrictions and obstacles you must overcome before you win.

This chapter will show you how to accurately play to win, how to complete combinations, and how to acquire the 14th Mah Jongg tile. We'll also carefully and thoroughly go over everything you need to know in between.

The game begins with East (who has 14 tiles) discarding a tile face up, being sure he or she identifies it by correctly naming it. East now has 13 tiles.

The player to the right of East then picks the next tile connected to the broken Wall, places it immediately into his or her rack (see "Racking" on page 99), and decides to either keep it or discard it. If the player decides to keep it, another tile from the hand must be discarded. If the player does not want the tile, it is discarded. Discarded tiles must always be correctly identified. The next player to the right then picks the next tile from the broken Wall, racks it, and decides to either keep it or discard it. The third player to the right picks the next tile, racks, and discards, and so on around the table. You cannot touch, pick, or look at a tile from the Wall until it is your turn. When all the tiles from one Wall have been picked, a new Wall is pushed to the center of the table. This new Wall comes from the player to the left of East. (Remember, new Walls always come from the left of East—clockwise, and picking tiles always come from the right of East—counterclockwise.) The game proceeds in this sequence of picking Wall tiles, racking, and discarding until one player declares Mah Jongg, or all the Wall tiles are gone and no player declares Mah Jongg. If no one declares Mah Jongg, it is called a **Wall Game**. At the end of a game, everyone throws the tiles back on the table, the tiles are mixed, a new Wall is built, and a new game begins with the next East.

As players pick and discard tiles, *any player* may interrupt the flow of the game and **Call** a tile. Calling is claiming a discarded tile from the table that's needed for the hand. Calling will be discussed in detail later on in this chapter. In Chapter 3, "Cracking the Code," we learned there are two types of hands, Exposed (X) and Concealed (C). Look to the far right of any hand on the card and you'll notice the designation X or C. Playing X hands allow you to call for a discarded tile followed by an Exposure (page 91). C hands do *not* allow you to call for any discarded tile, except the 14th Mah Jongg tile. Exposed hands and Concealed hands will also be thoroughly examined in the next section.

After a player makes a call and exposes, the game continues with the next player to the *caller's* right, picking the next Wall tile. If because a player has made a call, you miss your turn, so be it. Other players may call for other tiles until someone declares Mah Jongg, or all the Wall tiles are used and no one has declared Mah Jongg.

Do not discard when you declare Mah Jongg since you must have 14 tiles to win. (I can guarantee your heart rate will eventually return to normal.)

That's the way the game goes—picking, racking, discarding, calling and exposing to complete the combinations that you need for the hand you chose.

❧ How to Complete Combinations ❧

How do you complete combinations? There are three ways. Players may pick a needed tile from the Wall, call a discarded tile, or exchange a tile for a Joker used in an Exposure. We'll examine each one.

PICK A TILE

When it's your turn, you pick, rack, and decide that you want the tile. Just keep it, whether your hand is Exposed or Concealed. Then discard an unwanted tile. The needed tile can add to a combination or complete it.

CALL A TILE

Whenever you make a call, you are declaring that you want a discarded tile to use for your hand, and you are claiming that tile from the table. You must then use it to either a) **make an Exposure** (see below) or b) **declare Mah Jongg**, discussed on page 98. *Any* player may call for a discarded tile *any* time during the game, even if it's not that player's turn. Interrupt by saying "Call" or "Take" or anything that stops the game. Or by saying "Mah Jongg" or just "Mahj." Here we'll learn the procedure to call a tile to make an Exposure.

Exposure

What is an Exposure? It is a combination (a **Pung**, **Kong**, **Quint**, etc.) placed **on top** of your rack, "exposed," so everyone can see it. Calling a tile to make an

Exposure has the following restrictions. The first restriction: the hand must have an **X** next to it, indicating that it is an **Exposed** hand. **X** allows the player to call tiles for Exposures.

The second restriction: the player may only call for the tile that was *just* discarded. Once a tile has been discarded and no one calls it, it cannot be recalled later on. It is **dead**.

A third restriction: the called tile must be used *only to complete a Pung, Kong, Quint or Sextet.* You cannot call for a tile just to add to a combination you have in your hand. You must already have two tiles toward a Pung to call for the third, or three tiles toward a Kong to call for the fourth, and so on. If you have only one tile toward a Pung, you cannot call a second tile to add to it or call a third tile to add to a Kong, etc. But you can use as many Jokers as you wish to complete your combination.

After the player calls for a tile to complete a combination, then he or she *must make an Exposure of that combination,* a fourth restriction.

To make the Exposure, the called tile is immediately placed face up on top of the rack (not in the rack), along with the rest of the necessary tiles from the hand that complete the combination. Then another tile is discarded from the hand, being sure it is correctly identified. Nothing else is exposed from any other part of the hand. Make sure the hand still has 13 tiles.

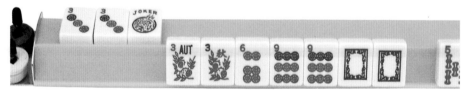

Exposure of a Pung

Exposure of a Kong

The next player to the caller's right then picks, racks, and discards the next Wall tile or has the option to call the previously discarded tile, if it is appropriate, and expose.

What about a Pair? *You may not call for a tile to expose or complete a Pair, except for the 14th Mah Jongg tile.*

Calling and Exposing with X Hands

1. Call, if your hand is X (Exposed).
2. Only the tile just discarded may be called.
3. Call to complete a Pung, Kong, Quint or Sextet.
4. Call is followed by Exposure of the Pung, Kong, Quint, or Sextet.
5. A tile to complete a Pair can only be called and exposed for Mah Jongg.

Correct the Exposure

If you make a mistake—say you expose a Kong instead of a Pung, or you expose the wrong numbers or the wrong Suit—you can correct your error and change your Exposure. If you call a tile and place it on the rack, but do not expose the rest of the combination, you may return the called tile to the table. You may even stop the game to call, and then after looking at the card and your hand, decide against exposing. (These are not good ideas, because you are giving your opponents information about a hand you may be considering. See Chapter 8, "Play to Win: Strategies.") There is no penalty for these missteps, but *once you discard, you cannot change or correct your Exposure.* As the game continues, you may want to change your Exposure, maybe add to it or subtract from it, but you can't. Once you have exposed and discarded, there is no turning back. So check your card and hand carefully before you call and expose to make sure you have the proper kind and the correct number of tiles.

But suppose you do make a mistake and expose incorrectly, discard, and realize it's too late to correct your error. What do you do? Nothing! You *quietly* look for another hand on the card that uses the same tiles you've already exposed. Do not announce your mistake to the other players. If no one catches your mistake, keep right on playing.

However, your hand may be challenged by another player, who must tell you the mistake you have made. If you agree the challenger is correct, your hand is declared dead and you can no longer participate in the game. You are further penalized at the end of the game, because you must pay the challenger the amount your hand is worth as listed in the **Values** column on the card. (You only pay if your group plays for money, of course.) If you disagree with the challenge, keep on playing. If, at the end of the game, the challenger was *not* correct, you get paid the amount the hand is worth from the challenger.

Remember, you can't change your Exposure once you discard. Consider before your first Exposure that you are making a commitment to play *that* specific hand. You should wait until you have at least seven or eight tiles toward a hand before you expose. In addition, you are giving your opponents some information about the hand you are playing. The more Exposures you make, the easier it will be for other players to determine your hand. I am not suggesting that you don't make Exposures. Just be aware of what you're doing.

Concealed Hands

If you are playing a hand with a **C** next to it, you have chosen a **Concealed** hand. You must pick all your needed tiles from the Wall yourself, or you may exchange a missing tile for an exposed Joker (see page 96) to add to or complete your combinations. But *you may not call to complete or expose any of your combinations. You may only call any 14th Mah Jongg tile.*

Calling and Exposing with C Hands

1. Only call for any 14th Mah Jongg tile, *including a tile to complete a Pair.*
2. Expose only a completed Mah Jongg hand.

All hands in the Singles and Pairs Section are Concealed and many require Single tiles. You may call any one of them only for Mah Jongg.

If you inadvertently expose a combination in a Concealed hand, you may be challenged. The penalty is severe. Your hand will be declared dead, you cannot continue to play, and you have to pay the challenger the value of your hand. Be sure to check the hand and the card carefully to avoid making that common mistake.

Concealed hands can be challenging and many times, frustrating. Beginners and, surprisingly, some experienced players shy away from them. So should you play Concealed hands or just stick to Exposed hands? There are advantages and disadvantages to both. Concealed hands offer the advantage that no one knows what hand you're playing. The disadvantage is that you cannot call for any tile except the 14th Mah Jongg tile. An Exposed hand offers the advantage of being able to call for tiles, but the disadvantage is that your Exposures reveal information about the hand you're playing. My recommendation is to play everything. Don't be dissuaded from playing a hand just because it's Concealed. Many times the hand your tiles match is a Concealed hand and you are left with little choice but to play that hand. More importantly, many times you will be successful and win. Moreover, you will learn a lot from the experience.

Review and More About Calling Tiles

- ⊕ Call for any 14th Mah Jongg tile, including a tile for a Pair or a Single, regardless of whether the hand is Exposed or Concealed.
- ⊕ Although they can be discarded, no player can ever call for a discarded Joker for anything.
- ⊕ A discarded tile cannot be called to replace an Exposed Joker.
- ⊕ Once a tile has been discarded and no one has called it, it cannot be recalled. It is dead, unavailable to any player at any time.
- ⊕ When two players call for the same tile for an Exposure, the tile

goes to the player whose turn comes next. The same is true if two players call the same tile for Mah Jongg. But when two players call for the same tile, one for a Mah Jongg and one for an Exposure, the player who declares Mah Jongg takes precedence over the player who calls for an Exposure.

⬤ Call to complete a Pung, Kong, Quint or Sextet if your hand is X (Exposed).

⬤ A tile must be properly identified before it can be called, either for an Exposure or Mah Jongg. If it is miscalled, it must be properly corrected. There is no penalty for miscalling a tile as it is being discarded. However, if a 14th Mah Jongg tile is miscalled and not corrected, the game is over and the miscaller is penalized by paying four times the amount the hand is worth. The other players pay nothing.

EXCHANGE A TILE FOR AN EXPOSED JOKER

The third way to add to or complete a combination in your hand is by exchanging a tile for a Joker from anyone's Exposure, including your own, even if you are playing a Concealed hand. The Joker then becomes part of your hand.

Jokers may be used in Exposures. But if you use Jokers, any player may replace your Joker with the appropriate tile to use in his or her hand. There are several situations in which this exchange can occur.

Here's an example. You have exposed a Kong of 3-Craks, using a Joker.

⬤ Situation 1. Another player picks a 3-Crak from the Wall.
That player can now exchange the 3-Crak for the Joker, place the Joker in his or her hand, and then discard.

⬤ Situation 2. A player has an unneeded 3-Crak in his or her hand.
First, the player must pick a tile, rack, then exchange the 3-Crak for the Joker, place the Joker in his or her hand, and discard.

⬤ Situation 3. You pick the missing 3-Crak from the Wall yourself.
You may then exchange the 3-Crak to take back your own Joker, and discard to finish the exchange.

If you have the missing tiles, you may exchange as many Jokers from as many Exposures as you wish.

> *Tip:* You do not expose anything from your hand whenever you exchange tiles for Jokers.

Note: When you exchange a tile for a Joker in an Exposure, you may actually be helping your opponent. Since you can't see the rest of his or her hand, the player may be on the way to a Jokerless hand (page 98). Just be aware.

Pay attention to Exposures and keep your eyes open because once you discard, that play is over and you (or anyone else) cannot call back the tile that you could have exchanged for a Joker!

Summary of How to Add To or Complete Combinations

💠 **Pick** a tile from the Wall.

💠 **Call**, only if your hand is Exposed.

   a. You can call only for the immediately discarded tile.

   b. You can only call to complete a Pung, a Kong, a Quint or a Sextet, not add to it.

   c. After you call a tile to complete your combination, you must expose it. You may use Jokers.

Once you discard, you cannot change your Exposure.

💠 **Exchange** a tile for an Exposed Joker, whether your hand is Exposed or Concealed.

   a. First, pick a tile from the Wall and rack it.

   b. Then, make the exchange.

   c. Finally, discard.

❧ Declaring Mah Jongg ☙

We have thoroughly discussed how to complete combinations in Exposed hands and Concealed hands. Acquire the 14th Mah Jongg tile the same way you acquire tiles to complete combinations. **Pick** the 14th Mah Jongg tile from the Wall, **call** any 14th Mah Jongg tile, or **exchange** a tile for a Joker from anyone's Exposure, including your own, and use it as the 14th Mah Jongg tile. Do not discard when you declare Mah Jongg.

We learned you cannot call a tile for a Pair to expose it, but you *may* call it for Mah Jongg. The same is true for the combination NEWS or 2004 or in hands of the Singles and Pairs Section. You may not call for any one of the missing tiles for an Exposure, but you *can* call the missing tile to declare Mah Jongg, whether your hand is Exposed or Concealed.

THE USE OF JOKERS

We learned that Jokers can be used to substitute for any and all Suit tiles, Dragons, Flowers, or Winds in a Pung, Kong, Quint, or Sextet, whether your hand is Concealed or Exposed. You may use as many Jokers as you wish in these combinations—up to three Jokers in a Pung, up to four Jokers in a Kong, up to five Jokers in a Quint and up to six Jokers in a Sextet.

There are a few additional rules regulating Jokers' use in play. Let's go over them.

You may discard Jokers. It's the safest discard because no player can ever call for a discarded Joker.

Once again, *Jokers can never be used in a Pair or to substitute for a Single tile.*

If you declare Mah Jongg without using Jokers, it's called a **Jokerless hand** and you must indicate it by declaring that your hand is Jokerless. You earn a bonus from everyone, which is double the amount in the Value column on the card. With a Jokerless hand, the player who discards your Mah Jongg tile is penalized and pays you double-double or four times the amount the hand is worth. If you pick your own Joker-less Mah Jongg tile ("Self-picked"; see below), everyone pays you double-double. Since the Singles and Pairs Section does not permit the use of Jokers, you don't get a bonus for a Jokerless hand.

When your hand contains one or more Jokers, there is no bonus. In that case, the player who discarded your Mah Jongg tile is penalized and pays you double the amount shown in the Value column. Everyone else pays only what is shown.

> *Tip:* Don't expose or throw your hand in when someone declares Mah Jongg until his or her hand is verified. The player may have made a mistake. In that case, the hand is declared **dead**. The player does not participate in the game any longer, replacing the tiles exposed for Mah Jongg back into his or her rack. If there are any Exposures with Jokers that were exposed before the incorrect Mah Jongg was declared, they remain exposed on top of the rack, and are free to be exchanged by any player with the proper tiles. The game continues with the remaining players. Any **dead** player pays the winner, just like everyone else.

SELF-PICKED MAH JONGG

Self-picked Mah Jongg occurs when a player picks the 14th Mah Jongg tile from the Wall (as opposed to calling for it). When you Self-pick a tile that gives you Mah Jongg, you get a bonus. You are entitled to be paid double the amount in the Value column by everyone else. The same applies when you exchange a tile for a Joker from an Exposure that makes the 14th Mah Jongg tile. The exchange can even be from your own Exposure. This is important because when the exchange leads to Mah Jongg, it is considered to be a Self-picked Mah Jongg and therefore entitles the player to the bonus.

✥ Racking ✥

Racking means that as soon as you pick a tile from the Wall, you immediately place it in your rack. Not on top of your rack or in front of your rack, but place it in your rack, next to the other tiles. Don't hold the tile in your hand. Don't think about it. Don't even bother to look at it. Until you rack the tile, another player may call for the tile just discarded. That discarded tile may be essential for someone else's hand or may even be the Mah Jongg tile for someone and you don't want to give that player a chance to call it. Get into the habit of racking your tile. It's very important.

By now you can see why we started our journey with learning about the tiles and progressed through the other steps of the game so we could more fully understand its complexities. The principle of the game is simple but its execution can be complicated. Let's review the seemingly simple procedures of the game.

Summary of the Game

- After building and breaking the Wall, selecting the tiles, deciding on a tentative hand, completing the Charleston, and completing Courtesy, East begins the game, discarding a 14th tile.

- Players, from right to left, *pick* tiles from the Wall, *rack*, and *discard*.

- When new Walls are needed, they come from the left of East.

- Any player, playing an X hand, may call for an immediately discarded tile to complete a Pung, Kong, Quint or Sextet, expose it, then discard. Play resumes to the right of the caller. Other players may call for other tiles.

- Players playing C hands may not call for any tile, except the 14th Mah Jongg tile.

- Any player may exchange Jokers for missing tiles in any Exposure, after first picking from the Wall.

- Do not discard when you call for or pick the 14th Mah Jongg tile.

- If no one wins, it is called a Wall Game.

✍ Changing Your Hand ✍

Mah jongg is wonderful fun! It's exciting and challenging all at once. But the real excitement and challenge comes not from the mechanical aspects of the game, like building the Wall or learning what X and C mean, or the rules of calling. Those are only the vehicles to get you to the skill (and thrill) of playing and winning! The fun and excitement come from being able to use the knowledge and skills you've learned to overcome the challenges presented to you in the game, whether from other players' hands or from the hand you are playing. So the actual playing of the game is where the real excitement is.

Much of the skill of playing mah jongg is about becoming a quick change artist. The challenge you will be confronted with is the need to change your hand, *quickly and quietly.* A frequent phenomenon in American mah jongg, it is part and parcel of the game. Hunting for a new hand can be daunting and many times frustrating. If you ask for "a minute," the other players quickly become aware of your situation. When you spend minutes scrambling for another hand, sometimes players become annoyed or bored (or both) waiting for you. More importantly, it reveals a poor grasp of the hands which, in turn, reveals a fundamental weakness in your game.

You can see why you need to know which hands on the card use some of the same tiles you already have. You may be sick of my mantra, "Know the hands on the card," but I don't know how else you can achieve any degree of success, except to know the hands on the card. There is no substitute for this number-one skill. The more you play, the more you will see the value of knowing the hands, especially if your goal is to win!

WHEN TO CHANGE YOUR HAND

Timing is everything! We've all heard that cliché before. But when to change your hand can be a critical decision. Waiting too long may not allow you an opportunity to complete your hand because many of your needed tiles are already out. Changing your hand too soon can lead you to lament, "I should have stayed with my hand." Unfortunately, there are no hard and fast rules here, but you should begin to assess the situation when the game is about half over. If your chosen hand is not happening by then, you will want or need to consider changing your hand.

There will be situations when it's obvious that you need to change your hand. In these cases there's not much else you can do. And then there will be situations when it's not so obvious. The question "Should you change your hand or not?" is a judgment call. Fortunately, there are some guidelines that can help you decide.

Here are obvious situations you'll surely encounter which necessitate a change of hand: the crucial tiles for your hand are discarded before you can call, because the hand is concealed or you have an insufficient combination or you just weren't paying attention; you incorrectly exposed; another's Exposure reveals tiles you need (especially tiles for a Pair); and frequently, you pick a tile that offers you another, better hand.

These situations are *not* obvious: Often, a player loses confidence in the chosen hand because one or more needed tiles goes out—especially in the beginning of the game—and rushes to find viable alternatives. *Don't* panic. Keep mental track of the discarded tiles, the Exposures made by your opponents, and how close the game is to its end. Keep the focus on your hand until you can see all its options are gone. You could pick the missing tiles; and remember, there are Jokers! Don't give up on your hand too soon. When your tiles offer so many excellent possibilities that you find it difficult to decide on a hand, be aware that you cannot keep *all* your options open and hope to win. *Keeping too many options open is a recipe for loss!* And many times, a hand isn't shaping up as you wish.

How do you decide? *Look* and *think!* See if you have enough picks from the Wall to possibly win. If most of the Wall is gone, your chances of winning are slim. Check the discards. Keep track of how many and what needed tiles are already discarded. Even if some of your tiles are discarded, you can still use Jokers. How many Jokers do you have and how many can you see exposed? Since there are eight Jokers in a set, if six are already out, the odds of picking one are slim. If you need a Pair you can't complete, look for a hand that requires a Pung or Kong of the same tile as the Pair. Do you have the proper number of Suits? Is one hand Exposed and one hand Concealed?

And consider the critical factor—the Pairs that the hand requires. Compare how many Pairs you need for each hand, because some hands require three Pairs and some hands require none. After weighing all these factors, then make your decision. Sometimes you **can and should** change your hand and sometimes you **can't and shouldn't**.

Remember, if and when you decide to change your hand, generally change to the hand that utilizes the greater number of tiles; contains the required Pair or Pairs; requires no Pair vs. one or more Pairs; can use Jokers in many combinations; is X as opposed to C; uses the same tiles but in different combinations. (Ex.: One hand requires a Pair, another hand requires a Pung of the same tiles or vice versa.)

When you are faced with situations when you can't change your hand no matter what, remember, nobody wins 'em all! As you gain experience playing the game, your confidence and skill will increase to recognize and better assess when you should or could change your hand.

So what do you do when you can't change your hand and you can't win? *Play defensively!* In the next chapter, "Play to Win: Strategies," you will find invaluable information about this aspect of the game.

❧ Betting ❧

Many players like to know about how you bet in mah jongg. Betting occurs if you have an outside person, most often a fifth player who rotates into the game. The bettor observes all the hands at the end of the Charleston and chooses which hand he or she thinks stands the best chance of winning. That player's name is written down where no one else can see it. If that player wins, the bettor gets paid the same amount the winner gets from the other players. If that player doesn't win, the bettor pays other players what everyone else pays the winner.

Try to play consistently—once a week (or more), twice a month, or whatever. The more regularly you play, the sooner you will begin to notice improvement. The more familiar you are with the card, the hands, and the rules of the game, the more fun you will have.

Speaking of the rules, in each chapter we have discussed the pertinent rules. If you need to refresh your memory, consult the back of the card, which contains many of the rules we discussed.

The next exercise, "Solitaire Mah Jongg," shows you how to play by yourself so you can practice, practice, practice all the things we've covered so far. It's very helpful and it's fun. The last quiz also offers you an opportunity to solidify the information we've just discussed.

We have almost reached the last stop on our journey. Now that you know the basics, you need a most important tool—simple and fundamental strategies. So on to the next and last chapter, "Play to Win: Strategies."

❧ EXERCISE ☙
Solitaire Mah Jongg

Here is an exercise that will sharpen your skills, aid in your knowledge of the card, and give you an opportunity to gain experience playing the game.

Mix the tiles and randomly select 13 tiles. Tentatively select your hand, do the Charleston by randomly selecting three tiles (except Jokers) and passing three tiles. Do this seven times.

Pick and discard tiles until you make the hand you've chosen. Be sure to read and follow the printed Instructions on the card to make sure you are playing correctly. Do this exercise again and again. It is an invaluable way to help you become a successful mah jongg player. And have *fun!*

⚬ QUIZ ⚬
The Play's the Thing

1.   Describe how the play of the game begins.
2.   How many tiles do you need for Mah Jongg?
3.   Can you call for a discarded Joker?
4.   When can a player call for a tile?
5.   What is racking? Why is it important?
6.   True or false? You can call for a tile even though it is not your turn.
7.   How many Jokers can you use in a Pung? A Pair? In NEWS?
8.   As the game progresses, you realize you need a tile that has already been discarded. Can you call for that tile?
9.   You're playing a hand with a C next to it; what does it mean?
10. What is the advantage of playing a Concealed hand?
11. You need a Pung of 5-Craks. You have two Jokers but no 5-Crak. Someone discards a 5-Crak. Can you call it?
12. What is the advantage of exchanging a tile for someone else's exposed Joker? Why might you not want to exchange that tile for a Joker?
13. Can you call for a tile to complete a Pair?
14. If your hand is declared dead, what does it mean?
15. What is a Wall Game?
16. You have made an Exposure mistake. Can you correct it?
17. Can you use 2 Jokers for a Pair?
18. Describe the process of exchanging a tile for a Joker.
19. What is an Exposure? Describe the procedure of calling.
20. What is a Self-picked Mah Jongg hand?
21. What are the three ways to complete your combinations?
22. Can you call for a tile to exchange for a Joker?

ANSWERS

1. East discards the 14th tile and correctly names it.

2. You need 14 tiles to declare Mah Jongg.

3. No.

4. Any player can call for a tile anytime during the game, if the hand is an Exposed hand, to complete a Pung, Kong, Quint, Sextet, or any 14th Mah Jongg tile—regardless of whether the hand is X or C.

5. Racking means immediately placing the tile you have picked from the Wall into your rack. As soon as you rack your tile, no player can call for a discarded tile.

6. True.

7. Up to three. None. None.

8. No.

9. Your hand is Concealed. It means you may not call for any tile, except the 14th Mah Jongg tile.

10. No one knows the hand you're playing.

11. Yes. Then you must expose the Pung of 5-Craks.

12. You may use that Joker for your own hand, but it might be helping your opponent to declare a Jokerless hand.

13. Yes, but only when it is the 14th Mah Jongg tile, in either an Exposed or a Concealed hand.

14. A dead hand does not participate in the game.

15. A Wall Game occurs when no one declares Mah Jongg.

16. Yes. You may correct your mistake as long as you have not yet discarded another tile from your hand.

17. No.

18. First it must be your turn, next you pick a tile from the Wall and then make the exchange. You may exchange more than one Joker, if you have the proper tiles to substitute. Then you discard from your hand.

19. An Exposure occurs when a Pung, Kong, Quint or Sextet is placed up on a player's rack for the other players to see. An Exposure may contain Jokers. An Exposure must always follow a call. A just-discarded tile may be called only to complete a Pung, Kong, Quint or Sextet by any player at any time, by saying "Call" or "Take," and then exposing their completed combination, only when the hand is X.

20. A Self-picked Mah Jongg hand occurs when you pick the 14th Mah Jongg tile yourself, either from the Wall or by using a Joker from any Exposure, including your own.

21. Pick a tile from the Wall, call a tile, or exchange a tile for an exposed Joker.

22. No. You can only exchange a tile for a Joker either by picking the missing tile from the Wall or by having the missing tile in your hand.

◈ CHAPTER 8 ◈

Play to Win: Strategies

Now it's time to turn our attention to the strategic aspects of the game. So get ready to sharpen your skills and turn to where the action is. Remember, your goal is to win but, barring that, your other goal is to keep others from winning and this chapter will provide some techniques to help you achieve both.

Some people say mah jongg is all luck. I don't subscribe to that philosophy. Yes, there is an element of luck, but it's what you do with what you have that's important. There's not much we can do about luck. But using skills and strategies will turn luck into wins. Knowing when to do what, observing what other players discard, keeping track of what tiles have been discarded, noting what tiles have not been discarded, observing what Exposures have been made and what information they have provided, are some of the essential skills that provide you with clues that will help you to win, or to keep the others from winning. The better able you are to pick up the hints other players provide, sometimes inadvertently, the better a player you will become.

As you play, you will begin to see how important strategies are. Your success depends, to a large extent, on the strategies you use—and strategies assume a firm knowledge of the hands on the card. Without that knowledge, these strategies will be of no consequence.

Beginning players often have the idea that if they separate their tiles into Pairs, Pungs or Kongs, they can see the hand they've chosen more easily. That may be true, but no experienced player separates his or her tiles in the rack. Why? Because it gives the other players a clue about the status of the hand. Players who keep discards separate from the rest of the hand inadvertently reveal to the opponents how close they are to Mah Jongg or whether they need a single tile to complete a Pair or Pung or Kong, and so on. Don't help your opponents. *Don't separate your tiles!*

Beginners concentrate a lot of their energy and focus on the card in order to keep track of the hand they are playing, and don't pay attention to what is going on in front of them. As a consequence, the game moves slowly, and important events are missed, such as discards and Exposures other players make. *Don't continually concentrate on the card or your hand. Focus on the tiles you need to complete your hand and that you can call.* You should know how many 3-Bams you need, if you can use Jokers, which tiles are missing, and so on. *Watch the discards and keep count of the tiles you need that have been discarded.*

Rack your tile immediately! Keep other players from calling for a discarded tile they may need for an Exposure or Mah Jongg.

Keep count of your tiles. Be sure you pick and discard correctly and in turn. If a player challenges you on the number of tiles you have, holding too many or too few can lead to your early demise.

Exposures reveal information; use it. When a player has made an Exposure, try to figure out what hand is being played. Here again, the importance of knowing the hands on the card is of paramount importance. The numbers (odds, evens, consecutive, 3s 6s 9s), whether the Exposure is a Pung, Kong, or Quint, and how many Flowers or Winds have been exposed, all give you clues to the specific hand. One Exposure might not tell you much because several hands may require the tiles exposed. But two Exposures will surely reveal more information and you should be able to hone in on the one or two hands that fit. Once you determine the hand, *do not discard tiles the player may need. If the hand requires a Pair, try to discard that tile early,* because a tile to complete a Pair can only be called for Mah Jongg. You hope to discard it before the player is ready to declare it.

Often Jokers are used to complete the Exposure. And it's a good idea— sometimes. Just remember that *any Jokers used in an Exposure become free for any player to exchange for the missing tile.* Also remember that *if you exchange a Joker for the missing tile, you may be helping that player towards achieving a Joker-less hand.* On the other hand, you could pick the missing tile from your own Exposure and take back your Joker.

Scenario: You have a Pair of unnecessary tiles in your hand. You discard one and hope another player will call it and use it with a Joker. The plan is that when it's your turn again, you can exchange the second tile for the Joker. Sometimes this strategy works. If it isn't called, you might assume the tile is *safe* (see next page) and discard the second one. Be aware that the player may not have called the first discarded tile, but instead waited for the second.

Use your Jokers to their best advantage. What do I mean? Let's say you have two Jokers and your hand calls for a Pung of something and a Kong of something else. You have one tile toward the Pung and two tiles toward the Kong. Don't use the two Jokers to complete the Kong. Use one Joker for the Pung and one for the Kong. Then you can be ready to call a tile to complete either combination.

Try not to expose too early in the game. Your Exposure gives clues to your opponents about what hand you may be playing. They may not discard other tiles you need. *Count how many of the tiles you need have already been discarded.* Sometimes, as I explained above, if you let the first tile you need go, another player may discard the same tile, thinking it is safe and then you can call it. Many times you will pick the tile you need yourself.

Don't expose unless you have to. Let's say you need a Kong of some tile and a player discards the fourth tile. Of course you call it. You have to. But many times you have a completed combination in your hand that contains a Joker. Someone discards the tile that you can use in that combination and you think you might use the Joker for a different combination. Do you have to call it? Yes, if it is critical to your hand. No, if it's fairly early in the game. Wait to see if you can pick the tile you need yourself or call when the Joker you use cannot be exchanged by the other players. Whenever you call and expose, you are giving your opponents information about your hand, so be judicious about your Exposures.

In addition, sometimes your Exposure reveals tiles another player needs for his or her hand. If it's early in the game, that player then has an opportunity to change his or her hand and has the possibility of declaring Mah Jongg.

Will you need to expose Jokers? How many? It's usually not a good idea to expose more than one Joker in an Exposure, especially early in the game. The more Jokers you expose, the more likely some other player will be able to exchange them with the missing tiles. And what are the chances of picking the tile yourself? Think before you expose.

Beginning players are usually anxious to call a needed tile for an Exposure. It's fun to use new skills. But sometimes a player has a change of mind, stops the game, and after review of the card and the hand, decides for reasons unknown, not to call after all. Try to avoid these situations, because you have just freely given opponents some information about your hand. They may not discard that tile again or they *may* discard the tile immediately on the assumption that you can't call—and once your tiles are out, you will not be able to win. Check the hand before you call to make sure your Exposure will be correct.

What is a safe tile? It's a tile no other player calls or a tile you know another player cannot call. For example, a player discards a 1-Dot and no one calls it. You have a 1-Dot in your hand or you pick a 1-Dot from the Wall. Discard it immediately after the first 1- Dot. The assumption is that no one wants it and it is safe. Or you have figured out what hand is being played because of the Exposures and you know a Pair of 1-Dots is required. If the first 1-Dot was not called, you can be sure the player cannot call the second. So discard it immediately and again, it is safe. A cautionary note is due here.

Safe tiles may not always be safe. A tile has been discarded and nobody has called it. The assumption is it's safe. But sometimes the player isn't ready to call, or is playing a Concealed hand, or doesn't want to expose yet, or needs the tile to complete a Pair for Mah Jongg. What was originally a safe tile now becomes *hot.* You can't always know that.

Don't discard a hot tile, if you can help it. A hot tile is new, one that has not been discarded during the game. Tiles become hot only when the game is about half over. In the beginning of the game, it's pretty difficult to determine what is hot and what is not. But as the game progresses, if a specific tile hasn't shown up, it may be because someone is saving them. I have seen it happen very frequently that someone discards a new tile near the end of the game and it is the Mah Jongg tile for someone. If you haven't seen a specific tile discarded and it's late in the game, it probably is hot. Sometimes you are waiting for Mah Jongg yourself and you have a dilemma. You must decide whether you want to keep others from possible Mah Jongg or if you want to risk discarding a hot tile to protect your own hand. Other times, from the Exposures, you know for sure you have the Mah Jongg tile another player needs. My advice is to play a defensive game.

Sometimes, the best laid plans of mice and mah jongg players go kaput. What do you do? When you can't change your hand, your tiles are dead, your hand is not improving, or *for any reason you can't win, play defensively to keep someone else from winning.* This is a very important strategy and one that you will find yourself frequently using, because many times you will find you can't win so your objective then is to keep your opponents from winning. Do whatever it takes—break up your own hand, don't discard a hot tile, discard safe tiles, and discard the safest tile of all, the Joker. Remember, if you discard the Mah Jongg tile for another player, you will be penalized by paying double for your kindness. What's the old expression? "The best offense is a good defense!"

Try desperately not to pass Flowers in the Charleston. But discard extra Flower tiles early in the game, if you're sure you won't need them. Get rid of them early but *don't discard them late in the game, unless you are sure they are safe.* Lots of hands require several Flower tiles, and many require a Pair.

Changing your hand is an important and valuable strategy that can lead to a win or a loss. It frequently occurs in the course of playing the game, as discussed in Chapter 7. There are situations when you have little other choice.

You will need to change your hand when:

1. The tiles you need are discarded before you can call.
2. You have made a mistake in your Exposure.
3. You need a Pair and your tiles have been discarded.
4. You're playing a Concealed hand and your tiles are out.
5. Someone else has exposed tiles you need, especially tiles you need for a Pair.
6. The game is about half over and your tiles aren't coming in.
7. You missed calling a tile that is critical to your hand.
8. New tiles offer a more promising hand.

When you need to change your hand, try to find another hand that uses the tiles you already have. Look in the Sections that use your tiles. Sometimes you can convert Pairs into Pungs and/or vice versa. And remember, there are many situations where you can use Jokers, even if your needed tiles are discarded or exposed. Don't give up too soon.

But there is a danger. Changing your hand frequently or excessively is not a good strategy to follow. Sometimes it seems like a good idea to change your hand because a couple of tiles you pick might go in another hand. And sometimes it is a good idea; as long as you have not come to decisive choice of a hand, tiles needed for the new hand are not discarded, and there are enough picks left in the Wall for you to create a winning hand, then "planning ahead" is reasonable. But if you keep lots of "maybe" tiles, tiles you "might use," the result is confusion, and deciding on a hand becomes overwhelming. So once you make a decision and have eight or nine tiles toward a hand, don't keep "maybe" tiles and don't be tempted to change. Stay with that hand.

But what if you have two potential hands? The question then becomes "Which hand should I choose?" How do you decide? Whenever you have a choice, always choose the easier hand. The X hand is usually easier to make than the C hand, as is the hand with the greater number of tiles. And be sure to check the discards. But the easiest hand to make is the hand that requires no Pairs. Since you know the difficulty in acquiring needed Pairs, unless you already have them, compare the hands' requirements and choose the hand that requires the least number of Pairs or the hand that requires no Pairs.

WHAT IF...

A player discards a Joker during the game, obviously an unneeded tile. It may mean several things: the player is waiting for a Pair to declare Mah Jongg, playing a Singles and Pairs hand, or going for a Jokerless hand. Be extra cautious about your discards. If there are Exposures, check the card to figure out which hand he or she is playing. If not, assume a Concealed hand. In any case, try to discard safe tiles.

It's fairly early in the game and you find your hand has rapidly improved and you are close to Mah Jongg, but you have a tile that you're pretty sure another player needs. Eventually you will have to discard it, if you are going to declare Mah Jongg yourself—sooner or later. Discard it sooner, rather than later. It may be the Mah Jongg tile for another player or it may not. But you will have to discard it and the sooner you do, the greater the chance of it not being the Mah Jongg tile. If it is, so be it, but know that you had to discard it eventually.

It's close to the end of the game, you only have a few more picks from the Wall, maybe two or three, and you realize you cannot win. Of course you want to keep your opponents from winning. *Discard the safest tile of all—the Joker.* The other players will probably be discarding Jokers as well. I know you are reluctant to part with your wonderful Jokers, but unfortunately, they are of little consequence to your hand at the close of the game and they can protect you from a loss and a penalty! You can't win and don't want to give your opponents a chance to win! Discard Jokers!

✿ ✿

These basic strategies will add to your game immeasurably and as you play, you will begin to develop some of your own. The more regularly and consistently you play, the faster your skill levels will increase.

And so ends our journey, with its many bumps, twists and turns. You started out knowing little or nothing about mah jongg, and ended with a discussion of some essential strategies of the game. Wow! You deserve *a big pat on the back!*

After you declare your first Mah Jongg and your adrenaline stops running and your heart returns to its normal rate, you'll really understand why mah jongg is such a great game. This book has introduced you to the vagaries, excitement, and challenges of playing the game of American mah jongg. *Now let the fun begin!*

✿ STRATEGY PRACTICE ✿

Here are a few situations that present a need to use a strategy that will help you to determine your move. Use the skills you've learned to answer these questions.

1. A player has exposed a Pung of 9-Bams. What information can you gather from the Exposure?
2. It's the beginning of the game and your hand calls for a Pung of 6-Dots. You have one 6-Dot and a Joker to go with it. A player discards a 6-Dot. Do you call it?
3. You need a Kong of Flowers. You have one Flower and two Jokers. Two Flowers are already out. A third Flower is discarded. Do you call it?

4. The game is almost over and you only have two more picks from the Wall. You are close to Mah Jongg but you need two more tiles to complete your hand. You have an unneeded Flower in your hand. It's your turn to pick and you pick a Joker. Do you discard the Flower?

5. You need one tile to complete a Pair to declare Mah Jongg. You pick a tile you can exchange for a Joker from some other player's Exposure. Do you make the exchange?

6. You realize your Exposure is a mistake. What do you do?

7. You are waiting for one tile to complete a Pair and one of your combinations contains a Joker. You have not made any Exposures yet and you could go for a Jokerless hand. Someone discards a tile that could be used in the combination that contains the Joker. Should you call it and discard the Joker?

8. A player exposes a Pung of 2-Crak and discards a 3-Crak. What might you surmise from the discard?

ANSWERS

1. Regarding the hand your opponent is likely pursuing, you can eliminate several Sections: the 2468, the Quints and probably the Year Hands. Look in the Consecutive Run Section. Do any of the 9 combinations require Pungs? Look in the 13579 Section and see if any of the needed 9s are Pungs. And finally check the 369 Section and the Like Numbers for a Pung of 9s. Now you have a better idea of the Section and perhaps the hand. *Then make a mental note of what the player discards.*

2. No. Wait! An important strategy is not to expose unless you must. You don't want to reveal information about your hand, especially if it's early in the game. You might pick the tile yourself. Others may think the tile is safe and discard another. Nor do you want to jeopardize your Joker while there are still missing tiles available to your opponents. So when your Joker is safe from being exchanged, call. *Expose only when you must!*

3. No. Wait. It's not a good idea to expose two Jokers in an Exposure. There are eight Flowers and you have four chances of picking a Flower yourself. Or wait until a couple more go out. Then you can call.

(Answers continued on next page.)

ANSWERS *(cont.)*

4. No. You shouldn't discard a Flower at the end of the game. Many hands require a Pair of Flowers and it could very well be the Mah Jongg tile for someone. In addition, you need two tiles to declare Mah Jongg yourself and other players will probably be discarding Jokers (if they're not, they should). At this point in the game, the possibility of picking two tiles for Mah Jongg or that someone will discard your tiles is close to nil. Protect yourself from discarding the Mah Jongg tile for another player and a penalty: *discard the Joker.*

5. No. The Joker is of no use for your hand and you may be helping your opponent to declare a Jokerless Mah Jongg. *Discard the tile.*

6. Say nothing and look for another hand or if you can't find one, *play defensively.*

7. If you don't call it, you are giving up the chance for a bonus (Jokerless hand)! If you do call it you are revealing information about your hand. Your discarded Joker tells your opponents you're waiting for a tile to complete a Pair. And for Mah Jongg. Just be aware, your Exposure may be enough for savvy players to determine your hand and not discard your needed tile. Then your only chance for Mah Jongg would be to pick the tile yourself. You can only use one tile for Mah Jongg so the possibility of someone discarding it is greater if no one has a clue about what hand you're playing. If you are a "risk taker" and it's early in the game, you might call the tile and expose thinking you have lots of chances to delare Mah Jongg. On the other hand, you might pick the missing tile yourself. So the answer is "Usually, no, do not call the tile you need for the combination, if it's early in the game." *Watch the discards.* If your needed tile has been discarded and no one has called it, the chance of it being discarded again is great.

8. You can determine that the Sections the hand might come from are the 2468, the Consecutive Run, Like Numbers and maybe the Year hands (depending on the card). Look to see if any hands call for a Pung of 3-Crak in the Consecutive Run Section. Why? If the hand called for a Kong, the player wouldn't discard a 3-Crak. If no hand requires a Pung of 3-Crak, then assume an even-numbered hand, Like Numbers or (possibly) Year hands. A second Exposure will definitely tell you more about the Section and hand being played. *And be sure to check the discards....*

Mah Jongg Sets:
Where to Purchase a Set & How to Update Old Sets

STANDARD SETS

You may see and purchase a standard American mah jongg set at:

www.americanmahjonggforbeginners.com

You may also e-mail your comments or questions about American mah jongg.

MAKING AN OLD SET USEABLE

Your set needs eight Joker tiles to be useable for American mah jongg. Unfortunately, sets manufactured before 1965 did not contain the necessary number. Sometimes people used the extra Flower tiles that came with their sets to convert into Jokers, but many times extra tiles were gleaned from other sets. These "Jokers" were converted by putting random stickers on them or they were sometimes marked with a blob of nail polish. These extra tiles many times did not match the sets they were used with.

Replacement tiles must always match the *back-side color* and the size of the other tiles of your set. Otherwise, you can easily tell which are the Joker tiles. If your old set does not have eight Joker tiles that match the back-side color and the size of your other tiles, you need to replace them with ones that match.

These replacements, called orphan tiles, may be available through the Internet; some sites to try are www.charlisstickers.com and www.mahjongtiles .com. The National Mah Jongg League also provides this service (see Appendix B). These sources also provide Joker stickers you may need.

❦ APPENDIX B ❧
How to Obtain Mah Jongg Cards

New cards are available from the National Mah Jongg League. When you request a card, you are automatically enrolled as a League member.

National Mah Jongg League
250 West 57th Street
New York, NY 10107
Telephone: 1 (212) 246-3052
Website: www.nationalmahjonggleague.org

New cards are available from the American Mah-Jongg Association.

American Mah-Jongg Association
8605 Snowreath Road
Baltimore, MD 21208
Telephone: 1 (800) 663-4581
Website: www.amja.net

GLOSSARY

Blind Pass is an action of the **Charleston.** If a player does not have the necessary three tiles to pass, the blind pass allows a player to add one, two, or three tiles from tiles just received to make the mandatory three tiles. The player may not look at the added "blind" tiles.

Breaking the Wall The roll of the dice determines the point in the **Wall** at which East separates tiles to begin the pick of tiles for a hand. The point of separation is where the Wall is broken.

C on the card indicates a **Concealed** hand. If the hand is Concealed a player is not allowed to **Call** for any tile, except the 14th Mah Jongg tile.

Call or **Calling a Tile** An action in the game when any player stops the game, "calls" for the immediately discarded tile to complete and expose a **Pung, Kong, Quint** or **Sextet** or to declare Mah Jongg. (See **X** below.)

Charleston The procedure at the beginning of the game by which players pass unwanted tiles to other players.

Courtesy A request for an optional exchange of one, two, or three tiles at the conclusion of the **Charleston**, with the player opposite. A player is allowed to refuse the request and not do a Courtesy.

Dead Hand The penalty that results if a challenger correctly finds a player has made an error in the number of tiles in the hand, miscalled Mah Jongg, or made an incorrect **Exposure.** That player can no longer participate in the game.

Defensive Play A strategy used to keep other players from declaring Mah Jongg.

Discard An unwanted tile taken from your hand, named, and placed face up on the table. A discarded tile must be correctly named.

Dragon Tiles There are three categories of Dragon tiles: **Red Dragon**, **Green Dragon** and **Soap Dragon**. There are four of each for a total of twelve Dragon tiles.

Exposure A completed combination of a **Pung**, **Kong**, **Quint** or **Sextet** placed on the rack for everyone to see. An Exposure always follows a **Call**. Also, when a player declares Mah Jongg, he or she places the hand up on the rack for everyone to see and exposes the hand.

First Left The last pass in the First **Charleston**. A **Blind Pass** is allowed on the First Left pass of the Charleston.

Flower Tiles depict versions of plum blossoms, orchids, chrysanthemums, and bamboo; some sets also depict ordinary people, which are also Flower tiles. (See **Mandarin Tiles** below.) There are eight Flower tiles.

Hot Tile A new tile that has not been discarded during the game that strongly indicates it may be needed by another player.

Joker tiles can be substituted for any and all **Suit**, **Dragon**, **Wind**, or **Flower** tiles in a **Pung**, **Kong**, **Quint**, or **Sextet**. There are eight **Joker** tiles.

Jokerless Hand is a completed Mah Jongg hand that contains no **Jokers**. A bonus is given for a Jokerless hand.

Kong Four matching tiles. **Jokers** are allowed in a Kong.

Last Right The last pass in the Second **Charleston**. A **Blind Pass** is allowed on the Last Right pass of the Charleston.

Mandarin Tiles have depictions of the "elite" class of people etched onto them. Mandarin tiles are **Flower** tiles. Not all sets have mandarin tiles. Usually, there are four mandarin tiles.

Matching Colors on the card indicate which tiles belong together to create the combinations needed to complete a hand. Matching colors require **Matching Tiles**.

Matching Dragon A **Dragon** that matches a **Suit**: Red matches Crak, Green matches Bam, Soap matches Dot. Also, on the card when the Dragon is the same color as the Suit, the Dragon is a Matching Dragon.

Matching Tiles are identical tiles of the same **Suit** and number, same **Dragon**, same **Wind**, or same **Flower**. They are:

Pair. Two matching tiles. No **Jokers** are allowed in a Pair.

Pung. Three matching tiles. Jokers are allowed in a Pung.

Kong. Four matching tiles. Jokers are allowed in a Kong.

Quint. Five matching tiles. Jokers are allowed in a Quint.

Sextet. Six matching tiles. Jokers are allowed in a Sextet.

Neutral Tile A tile that can be used with any other tile, regardless of the **Suit** or **Dragon**. **Winds**, **Flowers**, **Jokers** and **Soap** when used as a "0" are neutral tiles.

Pair Two matching tiles. No **Jokers** are allowed in a Pair.

Power Tiles are combinations of any tiles (Pair, Pung, etc.) including Flowers and Jokers. These are the nucleus of your hand.

Pung Three matching tiles. **Jokers** are allowed in a Pung.

Quint Five matching tiles. **Jokers** are allowed in a Quint.

Racks come with a set and are used to keep the **Wall** tiles straight, to hold a player's tiles, and to keep them hidden from the other players. Each American mah jongg set has at least four racks.

Racking Placing a picked tile immediately into the rack, thereby making it impossible for other players to **Call** for the immediately discarded tile.

Safe Tile A discarded tile that no other player will **Call**, or a discarded tile a player knows cannot be called.

Sections Categories on the card that designate the hands and describe the kind of tiles, numbers on the tiles, and how many of each tile are required to complete the hands.

Self-picked Mah Jongg occurs when a player either picks the 14th Mah Jongg tile from the **Wall** or exchanges a tile for a **Joker** and the exchange results in Mah Jongg. A Self-picked Mah Jongg results in a bonus.

Sextet Six matching tiles. **Jokers** are allowed in a Sextet.

Stealing See **Blind Pass**.

Suit Tiles There are three **Suits**: Dots, Bams, and Craks. There are 36 of each Suit—a total of 108 Suit tiles.

Wall is built by the placement of 19 tiles in two rows, one stacked on top of the other, for a total of 38 tiles in front of each player's rack. Players pick tiles, in turn, from the Wall.

Wall Game occurs when no player declares Mah Jongg and all the tiles are used.

Wind Tiles There are four Winds: North, East, South and West; sixteen Wind tiles in all.

X on the card indicates an **Exposed** hand that allows a player to **Call** for an immediately discarded tile to complete a **Pung**, **Kong**, **Quint** or **Sextet** and results in an **Exposure**.

$6.00

OFFICIAL STANDARD HANDS AND RULES

2004

麻雀

NATIONAL MAH JONGG LEAGUE, INC.

67th Year

Cut out the two pieces of the card (found here and on the next page)
and tape them together to match the picture of the full card on page 36.

2004   VALUES

FFF NEWS FFF 2004 (Any 2 and 4 Same Suit) . . . .**x 25**
FF GGGG 2004 RRRR (Kong Green & Red Dragon only, Any 2 & 4 Same Suit) **x 30**
NNNN E W SSSS 2004 (Any 2 and 4 Same Suit) . . . .**x 30**

2468

FF 2222 44 66 8888 or **FF 2222 44 66 8888** . . . .**x 25**
22 44 444 666 8888 (Any 3 Suits, Kong 8's Only) . . . .**x 25**
222 4444 666 8888 (Any 2 Suits) . . . .**x 25** ★
222 DDDD 888 DDDD (Any 2 Suits) . . . .**x 25** ★
2222 44 6666 88 88 (Any 3 Suits Pairs 8's Only) . . . .**x 30** ★
222 444 666 888 DD . . . .**c 35** ★

LIKE NUMBERS

FF 1111 1111 1111 (Any Like Nos.) . . . .**x 25**
FFFFF 11 111 1111 (Any Like Nos.) . . . .**x 25**

ADDITION HANDS

FFFF 2222 + 9999 = 11 or **FFFF 2222 + 9999 = 11** . . . . .**x 25**
FFFF 3333 + 8888 = 11 or **FFFF 3333 + 8888 = 11** . . . . .**x 25**
FFFF 4444 + 7777 = 11 or **FFFF 4444 + 7777 = 11** . . . . .**x 25**

Tape this edge to the other blue-starred edge.

Cut out the two pieces of the card (found here and on the next page) and tape them together to match the picture of the full card on page 36.

QUINTS

	VALUES
22 333 4444 **55555** (These Nos. Only)	X 40
NNNNN DDDD **11111** (Quint Any Wind & Any No. In Any Suit-Kong Any Dragon)	X 45
FF 22222 33 **44444** (Any 3 Consecutive Nos., Any 3 Suits)	X 45
FF 11111 + **99999** = 10 (Any 3 Suits)	X 45

CONSECUTIVE RUN

	VALUES
11 222 3333 444 55 or **55 666 7777 888 99**	X 25
111 2222 333 **4444** (Any 4 Consecutive Nos., Any 2 Suits)	X 25
11 22 111 222 **3333** (Any 3 Consecutive Nos., Any 3 Suits)	X 25
FFFF 1111 2222 **DD** (Any 2 Consecutive Nos.)	X 25
11 22 33 4444 **5555** (Any 3 Consecutive Pairs, Kongs Ascending Nos. Any 3 Suits)	X 30
11 22 333 DDD **DDD** (Any 3 Consecutive Nos. Any 3 Suits Pungs Opp. Dragons)	C 35

13579

	VALUES
11 333 5555 777 **99**	X 25
111 3333 333 **5555** or **555 7777 777 9999**	X 25
11 33 555 777 **9999** (Any 3 Suits)	X 25
FF 1111 33 5555 **DD**	X 30
FF 5555 77 9999 **DD**	X 30
11 33 11 33 55 **1111** (Any 3 Suits, Kong 1, 3 or 5)	C 30
55 77 55 77 99 **5555** (Any 3 Suits, Kong 5, 7 or 9)	C 30
FFFF **3333** X **5555** = 15 or FFFF **5555** X **7777** = **35**	X 30

WINDS – DRAGONS

	VALUES
FFF NN EE WWW **SSSS**	X 25
NNNN 11 11 11 **SSSS** (Pairs Any Like Odd Nos.)	X 30
EEEE 22 22 22 **WWWW** (Pairs Any Like Even Nos.)	X 30
NN DD SSS DDD **DDDD** (Pair Any Dragon)	X 25
EE DD WWW DDD **DDDD** (Pair Any Dragon)	X 25
NNNNN EEEE WWWWW **SS**	X 25

369

	VALUES
FFF 33 66 999 **DDDD**	X 25
FF 3333 6666 **9999** (Any 3 Suits)	X 25
333 66 999 333 **333** (Any 2 Suits, Like Pungs 3, 6 or 9)	X 30
33 666 DDDD 666 **99** (Any 3 Suits)	X 25
33 66 333 666 **9999** (Any 3 Suits, Kong 9's Only)	X 25
3 66 999 3 66 **999** (Any 2 Suits)	C 30

SINGLES AND PAIRS

	VALUES
NN EE WW SS 11 22 **33** (Any 3 Consecutive Nos.)	C 45
FF 11 22 33 44 55 **DD** (Any 5 Consecutive Nos.)	C 50
FF 11 DD 11 DD 11 **DD** (3 Suits Any Like Nos.)	C 50
FF 11 22 44 66 88 **99** (Any 2 Suits)	C 50
FF 11 33 55 55 77 **99** (Any 2 Suits)	C 50
FF 3669 3669 **3669**	C 50
FF 2004 NEWS **2004** (1 or 2 Suits, 2 and 4 Same Suit)	C 75

When a player Mah Jonggs on a discarded tile, **DISCARDER** pays the winner double value. All other players pay single value. When a player picks OWN Mah Jongg tile, all players pay double value.

BONUS: WHEN A PLAYER DECLARES MAH JONGG AND NO JOKERS ARE PART OF THE HAND, A BONUS IS GIVEN: DOUBLE VALUE. EXCHANGED JOKERS FROM AN EXPOSURE CAN MAKE THE HAND JOKERLESS.

EXCEPTION: SINGLES & PAIRS GROUP—NO BONUS.

STANDARD BASED ON EIGHT FLOWERS AND EIGHT JOKERS

Run—means consecutive numbers. **Pair**–2 like tiles; **Pung**–3; **Kong**–4; **Quint**–5. **1** color–any **1** suit; **2** colors–any 2 suits; **3** colors–3 suits. F–Flower; X–Exposed; C–Concealed; D–Dragon; R–Red D; Wh–White D; G–Green D. **Matching Dragons: Craks with Reds, Dots with Whites, Bams with Greens.**

Note: White Dragon is used also as **ZERO "O"**. It can be **USED** with any suit (Craks, Bams or Dots).

ALL TILES FACED DOWN AND MIXED. EAST ROLLS DICE and total number thrown designates where East breaks wall. Each player picks 4 tiles for 3 rounds. East then picks next first and third top tiles and other players one tile each.

CHARLESTON (FLOWERS MAY BE PASSED DURING ANY PASS INCLUDING COURTESY BUT JOKERS MAY NEVER BE PASSED)

First Charleston compulsory–three passes (right, across, left).

Second Charleston optional–three passes (left, across, right).

Blind pass of 1, 2, or 3 tiles permitted on last pass of either Charleston, without looking at them.

Courtesy pass–optional "0", 1, 2, or 3 tiles–with player opposite, whether one or two Charlestons are played.

Charleston is completed. East starts play by discarding 14th tile; players on the right of East play in rotation.

Jokers may be discarded at any time during the game and named the same as previous discard. Jokers may be used to replace any tiles in any Pung, Kong, or Quint only. Joker or Jokers may be replaced in any exposure with like tile or tiles by any player, whether picked from wall or in a player's hand, when it is player's turn. Joker or Jokers can **NEVER** be used for a **single** tile, or in a **pair**.

1. NO PICKING OR LOOKING AHEAD.
2. When two players want the same discard, one discard for an Exposure and another for Mah Jongg. Mah Jongg declarer always has preference.
3. When two players want the same tile for exposure, player next in turn to discarder has preference.
4. When two players want the same tile for Mah Jongg, player next in turn to discarder has preference.
5. A tile may not be claimed for Exposure or Mah Jongg after player next in turn has picked and racked or discarded a tile.

PLAYERS SHOULD NOT THROW IN HANDS UNTIL MAH JONGG IS VERIFIED.

MISCALLED TILE: A tile cannot be claimed until correctly named. Correctly named tile may then be called for an Exposure or Mah Jongg. HOWEVER, if Mah Jongg is called with the incorrectly named tile, the game ceases. Then, miscaller pays claimant four times the value of the hand. Others do not pay.

A hand is dead when it has too few or too many tiles during play or an incorrect number of exposed tiles. Dead hand ceases to pick and discard, pays same as other players.

At no time may a tile be called to complete a pair including flower for anything but Mah Jongg in an Exposed or Concealed Hand.

A discarded Flower may be claimed to complete a Pung or Kong or Quint of Flowers for Exposure or Mah Jongg in an Exposed Hand.

A discarded Flower may be claimed to complete the required number of Flowers for Mah Jongg in a Concealed Hand.

Player is permitted to discard a Flower at any time during the game and call it "Flower".

RULES FOR BETTORS: Bettor pays or receives same as player bet on.

MAH JONG IN ERROR

1. If a player declares Mah Jongg in error and does not expose the hand and all other hands are intact, play continues without penalty.
2. If a player declares Mah Jongg in error and exposes part or all of the hand and all other hands are intact, game continues but declarer's hand is dead. The same penalty applies for calling a discard or making an incorrect exposure. DEAD HAND DISCONTINUES PLAYING, DOES NOT PICK OR DISCARD. Pays winner full value of hand.
3. If a player declares Mah Jongg in error and one other player exposes part or all of the hand, the game continues with the two remaining players whose hands are intact. If more than one player, other than erring declarer, exposes part or all of the hand, game cannot continue. Erring declarer pays double the value of the incorrect hand to the one player whose hand is intact.

When writing for any information, please send a stamped self-addressed envelope to:

NATIONAL MAH JONGG LEAGUE, INC., 250 West 57th Street, New York, N.Y. 10107
(212) 246-3052 FAX (212) 246-4117 www.nmjl.org
Become a Member: $6.00 includes Score Card & Bulletin

Printed in the USA

Tape this edge to the other red-starred edge.